Drowned

Claire Tulloch

The characters and businesses in this book are entirely imaginary and bear no relation to real people, living or dead. Barley Cove is a real place but the author has taken liberties with topography, public transport and contemporary events for the sake of the story.

one

I'll never forget my fifteenth birthday, the fourth of November 1980, fishing with Dad in the river at the end of our garden. Draped over the rocks was a long-haired animal, the current burying the fur and then giving rise to it. Dad was adding bait to his fishing hook in the misty rain. I left my stool by the river, took a stick to steady me and waded into the water. There was a rag poking out and I thought the animal must be tangled up in it. The remains could have come from up stream. Maybe it was a cat who'd tried to catch a fish before falling in and being knocked unconscious before making its way down Hungry Hill. Last summer me and Jimmy Bray threw pebbles into this river. His dog picked up a bone from the gritty shoreline. It was long with knobbly bits on either end, like a cartoon bone, but brown and pitted. Me and Jimmy thought it looked like a shin bone. Ashley Tate had disappeared from our class about that time. There were rumours his mother had taken him to England, but I agreed with Jimmy when he said the bone probably belonged to Ashley, picked clean and thrown in by the Hermit on the Hill. This thing still had its skin on though. The hair was a mass of black. I poked my stick underneath to see if it would dislodge, but instead hooked the rag and lifted it. This bit of blue check was a sleeve – and at the end of it a white hand. I slipped, dropped the stick, and my back side hit the river bed. Water gushed into my trousers, weighing me down, then into my sleeves as I grabbed at the small rocks beneath me. The hand sank back into the water, but the blue check collar was now visible. The more I tried to get away, the more of the body I saw. The water lowered in front of me and the blue checks led to black shorts.

"Dad! Oh my God, help me!" I cried. The river clenched my waist with its cold claws, and rushed against me, keeping me down. Then Dad was behind me. He lifted me by my under arms, and guided me to the bank. "Dad! There's a body in the water there!"

Without hesitation he waded in and grabbed the blue-check collar to pull the lump, face down, to the water's edge. "Get to the house, get help," he directed, and I climbed from the shore to the rough grass-bank, to the end of our garden and through the back.

"Mam!" There was no reply. I dialled the station and breathed heavily into the receiver. "It's Tony Barber, come quickly, someone's drowned."

My father traipsed across the field carrying the flopping body. His waders swished through the grass and droplets of water leaked from the boy's hanging hair. My father's face was ruddy and his eyes downcast. Beads of water ran down his wax jacket.

"Did you phone, Tony?"

"I did, Dad. They said they'd be here soon."

The body's face was grey and swollen with two purple rings for eyes and a blue yawning mouth. Dad passed me and ploughed on ahead. The boy was laid on the lawn and my father went into the house. The hair was black, thick black hair like Jimmy Bray's. Jimmy was at school yesterday; he was probably there today too. If only he was still face down, then he could have been someone else, Ashley Tate, anyone, not Jimmy.

My father returned with a blanket and put it over the body.

"Go inside and make some tea, lad," he said.

"Dad, it's Jimmy isn't it?"

"Go and make some tea will ye!"

It was as if the river had seeped into my skin and was pushing to get out, warm and swollen behind my eyes. The heavy wooden door creaked and my muddy boots met the polished quarry tiles on the kitchen floor. No clean cups meant Mam must have been late for her dinner-lady job at school. The room was muggy. I removed my parka to hang on a worn oak chair and heard a car pull up. Through the front room window I watched Gardas Rafferty and Walsh alight from the police car. Rafferty covered his crew cut with his hat, Walsh looked up at the heavy sky and I saw his lips move. He reached to the back seat of the car and grabbed a navy raincoat. No police dogs.

They might think we did it. Nah. Why would either of us kill my mate Jimmy?

In the kitchen the tap water was hot. A cup slipped from my soapy hands into the sink. The clang startled me. Not broken, good. Mam's cuckoo clock chimed twelve-midday.

Please God, let that boy be out of here by the time Mam gets home from school. I moved the whistling kettle to a cool burner, and put four tea bags into the teapot.

We found this dead body, by the way Garda Walsh, how many sugars in your tea?

"Tony!" It was my father's voice.

The December snow blanketed the hilly farmland in blues and greys. Where we lived, in the cove, most of the snow had turned to slush. Dad turned up the car radio:

...has been shot dead by an unknown gunman who opened fire outside the musician's New York apartment. He was rushed in a police car to St Luke's Roosevelt

Dad shook his head. "I don't believe it, John Lennon is…" He lowered the volume and looked at me.

"Dad, you can say it."

"They say things come in threes. Let's hope this is the last of it for this year."

"Mam's going to be upset."

"There'll probably be Beetles music coming from the house when we get back."

We looked out of our windows.

"Maybe Jimmy will get to meet him," I said after a while.

"Maybe," said Dad, even though he didn't believe in heaven anymore.

"Will you open the gate when we get to the Brays'?"

"I will, Dad."

Dad smiled. "Probably best not to bring up John Lennon at the Brays'."

"No, I suppose not."

It was the first time I'd been to the farm since finding Jimmy in the water a month ago. Half of me expected to see him in the farmyard, clearing away snow or bagging dry feed for the cattle. The farm gate was heavy against the snow and I wished Jimmy was here to help me lift it – to make snowballs from the drifts against the hedge and pelt Dad's car with them when he drove through.

Jimmy's dad was still way off in the distance, carrying a shotgun over his arm. Behind him his minute prints trailed. After he had delved into the thick blanket before him he would come across our car, around it two sets of footprints.

Waiting outside the farmhouse was Jimmy's mother in her apron. Dad had sent a message yesterday to say we would be visiting. Jimmy's parents had no phone, Tom O'Leary delivered the message along with the peat.

A large bare tree stood behind the farmhouse, framing it. Yards away was the barn where Jimmy and I had played hide and seek on his fourteenth birthday last June. It was a sunny month and we had spent most of our time outdoors. Now the barn doors were closed to keep the animals in and the weather out. Dad stamped his feet on the mat to dispel all the imaginary snow he'd accumulated from the car to the porch. The sound was muffled as if we were locked inside a snow dome, waiting to be picked up and shaken again. The weather was taking a break, satisfied with what it had left.

We were ushered inside and our coats and scarves hooked onto pegs in the mudroom, which felt dank and unwelcoming. Inside the house was quiet and felt cool after the heat in the car.

"How are you, Mrs Bray?" asked Dad.

"I've been better, been better. Will ye be having some tea?"

"Ah yes now, thank you, Mrs Bray."

Mrs Bray disappeared through a dark wooden door, and Dad and I sat on the tapestry furniture looking at the lit candles and burning oil lamps strewn along sideboards and perched into cornices. I had not been in here before; I'd be surprised if Jimmy's mother even knew who I was. The farm was great to play on. Jimmy and I stayed well away from the farmhouse after Jimmy once said his father shouted a lot.

It was a ten-minute walk across the fields from our house to here. By car, it took fifteen, because you had to go right round the coast road and up into the hills. Today the farm felt miles away from anywhere, alone in our own little world.

Teacups rattled from behind the wooden door and muffled voices could be heard. The door eased open and in came Mrs Bray with a tray of teacups, teapot, milk jug and sugar bowl.

"Mr Bray is not long in; he'll be with us shortly." Mrs Bray busied herself and poured tea, adding milk and sugar, and then turned to stoke the fire.

"The rooms will be warming," she said. "For fear of wasting firewood I keep the heat to a minimum all day. To him it seems warmer than warm after being out in the cold. Fetch yourself a biscuit, Tony, they're in the kitchen."

I gently placed my china teacup and saucer onto the small round coffee table and pushed open the door I'd seen Mrs Bray come through. In the kitchen a leak dripped into a pail, its smell invading the room. The light was bright with snow reflecting through the window onto cleared surfaces, bar two limp rabbits that lay dead on a chopping board. Over in the corner, Mr Bray was peeling off his socks.

"Tony, God bless ye, how are ye?"

"Fine thank you, sir."

Mr Bray took a warmed pair of socks from the log-burning stove and dressed his feet before finishing off with his slippers. "Come into the sitting room," and I was led back to the adults, my biscuit still in the kitchen.

Mr and Mrs Bray talked, and Dad listened, saying something softly from time to time. It was occasions such as this I missed not having a brother or sister. Jimmy was more like my brother than my friend. Now

I didn't have a brother *or* a best friend. Who would I talk to? Everyone in my class already had friends. I watched the pendulum swing on the great grandfather clock and wondered what Jimmy would have to say about all this; the rosary beads hanging from his picture, a luminary portrait of the *Sacred Heart* and a flickering candle, declaring the mantle piece a shrine. The pendulum swung to and fro, one *Our Father*, ten *Hail Mary's*.

"Would you be interested, Tony?" Mr Bray was asking.

I came to when I heard my name. "Sorry, sir, I was thinking about Jimmy."

"Ah, well, yes. We need some help now see, what with Jimmy being an only one and all, it means my workload's doubled."

"We'd have waited 'til after the funeral to ask but what with the inquest delaying things. Don't misunderstand. It's not that we want to forget about him," Mrs Bray looked over to Jimmy's picture and made the Sign of the Cross. "The farm needs tending and we'd have to hire outside help if nothing else."

"Tony would be honoured," spoke Dad, on my behalf. I wasn't sure I wanted to help around the farm after school. Being there with Jimmy was one thing. The place was creepy without him.

Mr Bray was standing next to the fireplace pushing tobacco into his pipe. "We'll pay you well of course. See you round here tomorrow after school and we'll make a start."

Mrs Bray sipped her tea in an armchair and Dad looked at his watch.

"Well, best be off," said Dad. "Tony will arrive here tomorrow Mr and Mrs Bray, don't you worry."

"It's very kind of you," said Mrs Bray. "I'll fetch your coats."

<h1 style="text-align:center">two</h1>

There must have been over seven cats in the barn. Every day I saw a different coloured one dart from a hay bale and shoot through a hole in one of the stalls, back out into the dirty January weather. Mr Bray told me they won't let you pet them, farm cats, they're there to catch mice. I didn't mind working in the barn, it was warmer than fixing fences or searching for lost sheep. I'd always have to work with Mr Bray on those jobs. On my first day I ended up face down in a field after chasing a ewe and tripping over Mr Bray's dog. The collie limped her way back to Mr Bray and the ewe trampled down the fence and kept running. Mr Bray stood over me and frowned. I thought for a moment he was going to hit me with his stick. He took his pipe out of his mouth and said I'd be given no wages until the sheep was back in the field and the fence fixed. My parents taught me to respect my elders so I wouldn't answer him back. It was freezing tracking through the fields with a torch in the dark. Since then I always preferred to be left alone in the barn to muck out the horse, or clean her tack. Besides, I felt closer to Jimmy in here. Some evenings if the wind were whipping up I'd hear his voice saying my name. I could talk to him in my head about something funny that might've happened at school, and I'd hear him talk back – I knew what he was saying. I didn't mention this to Mam to Dad or to anyone. When I talked about Jimmy at home, things got strange.

If I walked into a room and they were talking about Jimmy, they'd change the subject, or Dad would usher me out into the shed and ask me to sort nuts and bolts into different boxes. I'd look at the fishing tackle propped against the shed wall and think about the day we found Jimmy. Dad and I didn't go fishing again after that day. I didn't ask him to take me again either. Mam was okay about not having fresh fish to cook anymore. The goose or duck Mr Bray would send me home with was good enough.

One night I thought I heard Mam say Mr Bray couldn't take it anymore. I imagined Jimmy's dad beating him like I thought he'd beat me when the ewe escaped, and holding Jimmy under water in a fit of rage, pretending it was an accident after he took it too far. It was always late at night when Mam said those things, as if she changed from being my mother into someone else. I'd wake up in the morning and the night before could have been a dream. Like the night I tried to fall asleep in my room with the radio on low.

Jimmy used to listen to the radio at night too without his parents knowing. The next morning at school we'd talk about the music we'd heard and the things the DJ said. We didn't have the money to buy the records, which was a shame. We reckoned if everyone who listened when we did went and bought the records the charts would be full of good stuff.

That night I don't think I heard any of what was being played or said on the radio. Listening without Jimmy wasn't the same. I smelled cigarette smoke and knew Mam must be upset again. I turned the volume on the radio right down and crept to my bedroom door. The floorboards always creaked under the window so I took a giant step over them. The catch never caught and was easy to open. The landing was dark except for the hall light downstairs. I sat on the top step and listened to the muffled voices coming from the living room. Mam was speaking very fast. Dad cut in enough for me to know he was listening to her. It was hard to tune in at first, then I heard Jimmy's name. I slowed my breathing in an attempt to hear more.

"There's nothing wrong. Leave it, will you," said Mam.

I stopped breathing altogether for a few seconds and closed my eyes. Mam's lighter clicked.

I heard Mam begin to cry. The living room door brushed against the carpet. I jumped back onto the landing and heard the front door close. The hall light clicked off and the living room door brushed the carpet again. I sat on the landing until the smell of smoke was gone.

Dad started spending more and more time at the hotel in the cove where he worked as a handy man. That may be where he went when Mam started crying in the night. I'd see Mam at school at lunch times, Mr Bray after school, Mam for dinner before I'd do my homework, have a bath and go to bed. I saw more of Jimmy's dad than my own.

We didn't go to midnight mass that year because Dad would've been too tired for working overtime on Christmas Day. Mam and I got up early Christmas morning and watched the television together as it drizzled outside. We listened to the Australians talk about the presents they had opened hours before us, the turkey they had eaten and the sherry that had made them squiffy. Their faces were tanned and red cheeked. In Australia I wouldn't have to go to places that reminded me of Jimmy, like the farm. Mr Bray said he could manage Christmas Day and Boxing Day but asked me to help clean up the farm during the holidays so everything would be in order by Jimmy's wake. Mam said no-one would mind if there was mud and hay in the farmyard but it was probably Mrs Bray worried more about visitors trampling the dirt into the farmhouse.

I'd been back at school a week when the news of Jimmy's wake came.

I filled the hay troughs and patted Jimmy's horse, Millie. Mr Bray whistled for his collie. It was time to bring the cows in for milking. I left the warmth of the barn and walked into the mist that promised frost before morning. Before long I was up to my ankles in thick mud. The beasts were being stubborn, refusing to go sweetly into their stalls without me first becoming filthy and receiving tuts from Jimmy's dad. *I* might have seen Mr Bray as more of a father recently; the cows weren't convinced I was his son. I wasn't Jimmy and those dumb animals knew it.

"You're the boss, not them!"

I moved into the milking area to fill the troughs with feed, leaving Mr Bray to herd the few last stragglers to their spots. Usually during milking Mr Bray and I worked silently. This evening Mr Bray was more vocal:

"Has the talk died down at school a bit?" he asked.

"Yes, sir," I replied.

"Seems the whole of Barley Cove has nothing better to do than lay speculation as to how our Jimmy died. Think they know better than them that's qualified. He'll be home tomorrow for the wake, then we'll bury him and that'll be that." He turned on the radio and classical music drifted into the sheds. It was a far cry from what me and Jimmy used to listen to. Mr Bray said his milk production doubled since playing music to his herd. The milking machines tugged in the background and a fresh tinge of pain surfaced as I worried about seeing Jimmy's dead body again tomorrow.

The next morning I closed my eyes when opening my bedroom curtains so I wouldn't see the river. At the Brays' Mam took my hand and led me to the coffin. It wasn't the same boy Dad pulled out of the river. His face had a matt look to it and his hair was dry and carefully combed. He was wearing the suit he'd been confirmed in, slightly shorter on the legs. His hands were in a prayer position and someone had woven the rosary beads from his picture around them. I wondered who had done it, whether the funeral parlour or Jimmy's mother. I'd not known Jimmy carry them in his pocket. It could have been a complete stranger lying in that coffin, compared to the boy pulled from the river. Mrs Bray served as a constant reminder as she wept over his body whilst women scurried around with trays. Dad took a glass of whiskey and finished it in one gulp. A large, square tin was shoved into my hand and I was told to make sure everyone had a biscuit. Jimmy's coffin was in the centre of the room, with its fake brass handles and white satin padding. To the left was a table full of sandwiches, cakes and bread baked that morning. On the other side was a table full of brandy bottles, whiskey in glasses and a jug of water. Five women were squeezed onto a three-seater settee. They chewed tiny mouthfuls and talked about their relatives.

The sandwiches looked cold and uninviting. I was empty with no appetite. Beth Harrington, the district nurse, was fussing around everyone, making sure there was enough to eat. Mr Bray sat in his armchair and sucked on his smokeless pipe. Cups and saucers littered the floor where people had run out of coffee-table space. The five on the couch had run out of small talk and sat in awkward silence. Jimmy's Uncle Tom spoke, and told the story of the Black Hound of Kildare and the time it had been seen running wild on Hungry Hill.

No footprints left behind. Like the devil it appeared and then disappeared as fast. A dramatic silence followed. The clink of a kicked cup against ceramic startled Mrs Bray. Beth Harrington produced a cloth and soaked up pale tea from the rug.

There was no school on the day of his funeral. The whole cove shut down apart from the hotel. Dad said he had to stay behind and hold the fort. I went to the church with Mam. It was still dark when we got there. The priest had organised a vigil in the presbytery. Women with black veils hung their heads over their rosaries and prayed for the dead. The smell of incense wafted through the small room. It was too much for Mam in the end. She grabbed my hand and we left to wait outside the church and watch the others arrive. The car park soon filled. I watched a Land Rover squeeze against a hedge at the side of the road. A group of boys climbed the stone wall surrounding the graveyard. Their mother slapped their legs and the boys started crying. Mam was fumbling in her bag. I pulled a tissue out of my pocket and she blew her nose. She started talking to Beth Harrington. Joe Harrington, the local butcher, was Beth's father.

"Hello Tony?" he said. His thick red hair covered with a hat. He scratched his beard.

I nodded and hoped he'd go away. He was the biggest of all the men in Barley Cove and his voice boomed. Beth was quietly spoken and Dad reckoned she was the prettiest of all the women in Barley Cove, except for Mam. Beth was the same age as Mam, and without a husband. Mam said Dominic O'Leary had asked Beth to marry him once. When Beth said no, Dominic went crazy and took his mother to live on Hungry Hill. He grew his hair long and stopped shaving. Some people said he was a wizard. Dad called him a hermit; he wasn't. He lived with his mother until she died. Mam and Beth went over to one of the benches to talk, and Joe Harrington started discussing business with another shopkeeper. I went to the car park to look around. A GB sticker on a sport's car caught my eye. The number-plate was British too. On the back seat there was a brown suede coat.

"Tony! Tony come on!"

It was Mam. I pulled up my collar and followed her and Beth into the church.

Mr Bray was kneeling in the front pew. I spotted Dominic O'Leary at once; his arm around Jimmy's mother, his white ponytail poking out beneath his leather hat. He looked over his shoulder at Beth whilst we genuflected and shuffled onto the bench. Beth quickly bowed her head before we knelt down and made the Sign of the Cross. I tried to pray, I really did. I started with the *Our Father* but kept thinking about Dominic with his arm around Mrs Bray. I leaned towards Mam and whispered.

"Mam, why has Dominic O'Leary got his arm around Jimmy's mam?"

"He's her brother. Now ssh and pray for Jimmy."

I closed my eyes. Dominic was Jimmy's uncle. I hadn't put two and two together before. All the times I joked about Dominic being a wizard and Jimmy had said nothing. I felt my cheeks flush. I opened my eyes and looked ahead a few pews. He had both arms around Mrs Bray now, her face buried in his neck. He was noble somehow; not the wild haired, crazy eyed hermit on the hill. The bells tinkled and we all stood. The organist opened the ceremony and we picked up our hymnbooks. I sang and looked at all the flowers. Pinks, purples and reds filled the floor beneath the altar. There was a picture of Jimmy on top of his coffin, and his name, JAMES, in white carnations. Jimmy had said when he was eighteen he'd insist everyone call him James. He'd always be Jimmy to me though. It was James that was dead. The hymn ended and we all sat. Jimmy's dad stood and bowed before Jesus before making his way to the parapet. Mrs Bray buried her face deeper into Dominic's coat while her husband spoke. I bowed my head when I heard her sobs. Mr Bray read the eulogy. I leaned against Mam and she put her arm around me. Mr Bray was telling everyone about the time Jimmy painted the inside of the barn bright red after finding an old pot of paint in the shed. We'd painted the barn together. Mr Bray had given us a telling off at the time, the inside of the barn stayed red though. The one decorated barn in Ireland we reckoned. Mam handed me a tissue and I realised I was crying. She hugged me to her. My friend was gone. I'd never see him again.

"It's not fair, Mammy," I said. "It's not fair."

"I know, sweetheart, I know."

Outside the church we waited for Jimmy's coffin to be brought through. Mam started crying and this time I put my arms around her. I glanced over at Cora who was in my class at school. She smiled and I looked away. I wanted to be invisible.

I held Mammy's hand when Jimmy was lowered into the ground. Mrs Bray could hardly stand and had Dominic and Mr Bray on each side to hold her up. It was mostly adults at the burial. I'd told Mam I wanted to be there even though Dad thought it was a bad idea. I'd not been to a funeral before. I was too little to remember my grandparents pass away. When I thought I couldn't cry anymore I'd hear someone sob and fresh tears would roll down my cheeks.

"His bed's in Heaven now, Tony," said Mam.

Joe Harrington gave us a lift back up the coast road to Mr and Mrs Bray's farmhouse. The coat pegs were so full in the mudroom, my parka slid right off. I dug beneath the coats and managed to find room and bundled my scarf into the pocket before I followed Mam into the living room. It smelled of cooked ham and sweet cream, like Saturday teatime. A fire crackled in the hearth and greeting cards stood in greys and mauves on the mantle piece, some with the Sign of the Cross in silver, all of them reading *In Sympathy*. The windows dripped with condensation and a haze of pipe smoke drifted around each lamp. People spoke in hushed tones and leaned occasionally over the table to pick a triangle-shaped sandwich or a slice of thick buttered soda bread. There was only standing room left for those who'd been to the graveyard, apart from Mrs Bray, who sat in the armchair by the fire, with Dominic on a stool next to her. Her eyes were red and puffy and she'd bring a handkerchief up to her nose from time to time. One of the women passed her a cup of tea. Mrs Bray stirred her drink absently before the spoon clinked onto the saucer. She took a sip and stared into the cup before using her other hand to wipe her nose again.

I felt a blast of cool air when the living room door opened and in came Dad.

"Hello, Tony, are you all right?"

"I'm okay. Mam's in the kitchen, she's been wondering where you were."

"I couldn't leave – everyone's here and we've no cover at the hotel." Dad smiled when a glass of whiskey was given to him.

"I'll go and pay my respects to Mr and Mrs Bray, then talk to your mother."

I watched him weave through the guests then made my way to the table for some food. I loosened my tie and undid my top shirt button, then collected a plate and serviette.

"You and Jimmy were best friends weren't you?"

It was Cora. I hoped she hadn't seen me crying in church. I nodded. "We were."

"I liked him, he was funny."

I smiled, not knowing what to say next. Jimmy had liked Cora, although he'd not told her. Cora was American and had been at our school since last September. I used to tease Jimmy I'd ask Cora out for him. I wouldn't have though, I was always a little afraid of her. She was confident and answered difficult questions in class. I worried she'd think I was an idiot. How was she related to the Brays?

"My dad used to go to school with Jimmy's dad, that's why I'm here," she said.

There was no one in the room I didn't recognise. "Which one's your dad?"

"Oh, he's not here. I'm here with my Aunty Peggie, I'm staying with her."

Cora looked over to her aunt who was in Dominic's seat beside Jimmy's mother.

"It's hot in here, don't you think?" Cora used her hand as a fan in front of her face. Her fingernails were bitten down.

"Shall we go for walk?" I said.

"That sounds a good idea, I'll grab my coat."

How I had the courage to suggest a walk I don't know. Perhaps Jimmy was leading me. By the time Cora reappeared I was glad we were leaving the mourning for a while. She was wearing a red coat and I noticed her black skirt peeking out as she led the way to the front. Girls rarely wore black here, not until they were old enough to leave home or be married. Cora took her gloves out of her pockets and I unhooked my parka from the peg and shut the door behind us. I wrapped my scarf several times around me and wanted it to cover my nose and mouth to stop the icy air getting in. We breathed like smoking dragons as our feet crunched the frozen mud beneath.

"How long were you and Jimmy friends?" she asked.

"Since nursery."

"Wow, that must be real nice, to have a lifelong friend."

I could feel tears starting to well again and I swallowed hard so Cora wouldn't see.

"I've never been in one place long enough to make any friends."

"Did you live with your mam and dad in America?"

"Yeah, mostly Mom. Dad's in the airforce and away a lot. We followed him around all over. I changed schools every couple of years."

"I've lived here all my life. Jimmy was my one true friend."

"We're not so different," said Cora, and she smiled at me again. Her teeth were perfectly straight.

We walked away from the house and were nearing the barn. "Come here, I want to show you something." I looked over my shoulder to see Cora following me. Her ringlets bounced golds and reds in the winter sun. I pushed up the plank that held the barn closed, then welcomed the warm smell of hay. Jimmy's horse neighed. I watched Cora look around.

"Hey, the red walls!"

I felt pride bloom in my chest. "I helped Jimmy paint it. Looks good, don't you think?"

"It does. What a great place. My aunt's cottage is small, I would love a place like this to hang out in."

"I come up here after school to help Mr Bray around the farm. Maybe you could come up too one evening."

After I said it I wished I hadn't. There was no way a girl like Cora would want to hang around a smelly farm with me.

"Not dressed in this," said Cora, twirling round to show off her coat.

"No, you'd need your wellies."

"Wellies, what are they?"

"Wellington boots."

Cora laughed and I noticed she had no black fillings. "I'll ask my aunt to take me and buy a pair of wellies."

It sounded such a silly word when she said it. I felt myself smiling again. I walked over to Millie and rubbed her neck. Cora took off her gloves and started looking round the barn.

"Hey, this must be some of Jimmy's stuff."

I left Millie and went to see what Cora had found. There was the football that Jimmy and I used to kick around together, on the flat pastures across the stream. I thought about the orchard beyond and how we'd steal apples afterwards, so ravenous we couldn't wait until we got home to eat.

"I'm sorry, am I making you sad?" said Cora.

"It's okay, I was remembering, that's all." I noticed a gap against the barn wall. "Something's missing."

"What?"

"I don't know." I pointed. "That space wasn't there before."

"Was it something big?"

I looked along the edge of the barn without knowing what I was looking for. I moved some brushes and forks aside. Propped against the wall was Jimmy's silver bicycle pump. "His bike."

"Maybe it's been put away."

"No, there's nowhere else for it to go. He always kept it here in the corner of the barn to stop it rusting outside."

Cora put her hand on my arm. I wanted to tell her everything I knew about Jimmy, in a way I couldn't explain to anyone else. I swallowed hard again before any tears could appear.

"We spent most of last summer doing up our bikes. I'd sanded the rust off all the chrome and Jimmy had touched up the paint work in our own colours."

"Don't worry, Anthony, we'll get to the bottom of it."

Cora's voice felt soothing and I let it drift around in my head for a moment. It was rare for anyone to call me Anthony, and out of habit I nearly said 'call me Tony'. There was something in the way she pronounced it though, the soft *th* that took away its harshness. It reminded me of the saint I was named after, Saint Anthony, the wonder worker, perfect imitator of Jesus, who received the special power of restoring lost things. I'd prayed to him and asked him to bring Jimmy back. Even though I knew that couldn't happen. Not long ago Mam lost her house keys; she mentioned it to Father Molony's housekeeper who suggested she should pray to Saint Anthony. Two days later Mam found the keys in the garden shed. She'd left them on a pile of old clothes whilst digging around for a spare fuse. Surely there'd be no harm in asking my saint to help me find the bike.

Cora moved her hand from my arm and I snapped back into focus.

"The bike was here yesterday," I said. "I remember hanging my hat on its handlebars before feeding Millie."

"It must have been stolen."

Back at the farmhouse the living room was a little emptier.

"Where have you been?" asked Mam.

"Outside with Cora." I gestured towards my new friend.

"Pleased to meet you," Cora said, shaking Mam's hand. "I'm Cora."

Mam smiled. "You're American. Are you Peggie Sheehan's niece?"

"Yes, ma'am."

I cut in before Mam started asking Cora too many questions. "Mam, Jimmy's bike's been stolen; it's not in the barn."

"Tony, this is hardly the time or the place. Don't go pestering Mr and Mrs Bray about it. Go and sit down and be quiet."

Cora and I went to sit on some dining room chairs around the edge of the room.

"Why don't you ask his uncle if he knows what's happened to it?" Cora tipped her head towards Tom O'Leary.

Jimmy's Uncle Tom was grazing at the food table. A glass of whiskey in one hand, his cheeks and nose looked warm and red.

"Wait here," I said to Cora. I pushed my tie back into place, went over to the table and picked up a dessert bowl. "Hello, Mr O'Leary."

"Ah, Tony, 'tis good to see ye."

It was odd seeing Tom O'Leary in a suit. He was usually in trousers and braces with a flat cap, delivering peat. He looked clean apart from the telltale muck underneath his fingernails.

"I was wondering, sir, if you knew where Jimmy's bike was."

Tom left the sandwiches alone and took a swig of his drink. He swayed a little. "Why are you asking about Jimmy's bike?"

"I was out for a walk earlier and went into the barn to warm up. I noticed his bike was missing."

"Sold," said Tom. "Now don't you be asking Mr and Mrs Bray about it, you hear?"

"Yes, sir. Sorry, sir." My insides gurgled. I wanted to shout over to Mr and Mrs Bray, *how could you be so heartless?* I left my empty dish on the table and went back to Cora. "They've sold it."

"Sold it?"

"They have, and not even asked me if I wanted it."

"Shall we see if we can find out who it's been sold to? Perhaps you can buy it back."

I felt my anger melt a little.

"We can't ask the Brays. We should go into town tomorrow and ask at O'Callaghan's bike shop."

"I can't tomorrow," said Cora.

I opened my mouth to speak and a loud crash stopped me.

"You drunk old fool! Look at ye."

Tom O'Leary lay on the floor with his legs covered by the linen tablecloth. A laugh jumped from someone's mouth and I saw Joe Harrington turn his back in embarrassment. Dad's feet crunched over bits of broken crockery and he helped Tom to his feet. Mam shook her head and went back into the kitchen.

"Jimmy's better off dead than living in this sham," said Tom.

Dominic and I exchanged glances, his eyes focused and cool. It was as if an invisible wave was travelling between us, trying to tell me something I needed to know. Dominic looked over at Tom.

"Tom, enough! Home for you." Dad wiped jam and cream from Tom's jacket. He put Tom's arm around his shoulder and walked him out of the farmhouse. Mam came back from the kitchen with a dustpan and brush and a cluster of women buzzed around the table like a swarm of bees. The stairs entrance slammed. Mrs Bray's chair was empty.

"What do you think that was about?" said Cora.

I shook my head. The women dispersed and the table was cleared.

"About tomorrow."

It took me a moment to remember what Cora and I were talking about. Then I remembered. "You don't want to meet me tomorrow."

"I do, but my aunt has got me sanding paintwork. She insists I do at least a couple of hours a day… *it'll be done before you know it.*" Cora mimicked her aunt's Irish accent and shook her head.

So, she really was busy. "What about later in the afternoon, say three o'clock?" I tried.

"Okay, that could work. How about we meet at the playground in Westwood?"

I nodded and wondered how she knew about the playground. Who'd taken her there? It was hard to find and dangerous to play on. Not many kids risked going, in case their parents found out.

"Shall I meet you there around three?" said Cora.

"Yes. I'll meet you there after I've been to O'Callaghan's."

three

There was no one in the bicycle shop when I entered.

"Mr O'Callaghan?"

"Come on up!"

Redundant hubcaps and screws congregated in corners of the wooden stairs. In the attic, tyres hung loosely from jutting nails. Yellowed boxes pressed up against the window and its paint-peeled frame. Mr O'Callaghan appeared from behind his workbench, his white hair wafted softly around him. His skin was so papery it looked like ash from burned wood, the kind which seems solid but crumbles if you touch it. He was wearing the same beige cardigan he wore last time I saw him. He pulled out a handkerchief from one of the huge pockets and blew his nose.

"How are you, Tony? Joe mentioned you'd be dropping by."

Mam must have told Joe Harrington when she came to buy her meat from him this morning.

"Fine thank you, Mr O'Callaghan."

"Will you have a seat?"

I hitched up onto a tall stool and O'Callaghan picked up a couple of spokes from his workbench and began twisting them together.

"I was wondering, Mr O'Callaghan, if you'd sold Jimmy Bray's bike yet."

"Jimmy Bray's bike now you say?"

"Hmm."

"If I'd have had it to sell I would've, the last time I saw Jimmy's bike, Jimmy was riding it. Must've been just before he died, riding to Joe's here with a couple of his dad's chickens."

"You weren't sold the bike by his parents?"

"No I was not, and if they'd have offered it me I'd have told them to keep the thing. Selling their dead son's possessions, well…" He turned to his workbench and felt around a scattering of metal oddments. "I'd say you'd best try Johnston & Son in Castletown. They might have sold it to him."

I thanked Mr O'Callaghan and jumped down from the stool.

"Funny business with Jimmy Bray," said Mr O'Callaghan thoughtfully. "I remember last summer I was walking along the sandy path leading past Bray's farm. It was a dusty road from the heat. I was crossing the bridge right where the water turns into a torrent. I saw Jimmy with a lad I didn't recognise in the wide pool there."

My insides lurched. Mr O'Callaghan continued:

"He'd waded in after a salmon trapped by the low water. I shouted to him 'you'll never catch that fish', and he shouted back 'I'll catch it with my bare hands'; and he did. I watched him catch the fish after a mad struggle. Took it home to his Ma and they had a fine feast I heard." Mr O'Callaghan turned to me. "How can someone who knew the water that well die by drowning I ask?" He took out his handkerchief and blew his nose again. "Give my regards to your parents, Tony."

"Will do," I said, and left Mr O'Callaghan with his bicycle wheel.

Jimmy hadn't told me about catching the salmon, nor the boy he was with. Why didn't Mr O'Callaghan recognise the boy? Everyone knew everyone in Barley Cove.

I kicked the bike stand back and looked at my watch before riding away. It was quarter to three. Dad was at work and Mam would still be shopping with Beth Harrington. I headed for the secret place where Jimmy and me always went, when the farm was too busy or my parents were arguing.

The smell of heavily creosoted wood hit me when I swung into the entrance leading me off the busy main road. The front brake on my Raleigh bobbed rhythmically on the tyre when I slowed to make the turn. Away from the shops, uniform houses stood block shaped, all with turquoise-blue doors and window frames. The rancid smell of cooking cabbage drifted past and someone hollered at her children. I ducked to avoid the low branches hanging over the hospital wall. Jimmy had been in there, laid out cold with a sheet over him. I wanted to be close to Jimmy again, let him know I felt betrayed about his secret friend last summer.

I passed the first empty playground with its iron apparatus that lolled like dry bones on a black-desert sand. We told our parents this is where we played. Westwood was at the bottom of Hungry Hill. We said to any soft kids who dared to come, they might be caught by Dominic O'Leary, the hermit on the hill, who roamed around his land in unlaced-hobnailed boots. I wondered if Dominic knew what everyone said about him.

The houses disappeared and so did the tarmac. It was milder today and the hard ground had given way to a muddy path. Chunks of chiselled-looking slate stuck out of the mud, forcing me off my bike to walk rather than risk a puncture.

Hawthorn and bramble started to tug on my parka as the path narrowed. There were crab-apple trees scattered all along the overgrown hedgerows and the sound of the clear, gravel stream twisting its way towards the sea. The entrance to the wreck was no more than a gap in the hedge. I dropped the bike stand, crawled through and batted bits of leaves and soil from my trousers. A boy ran past me, his shaggy blond hair trailing behind him. It was Peter Devlin. I followed him to the pulley. By the time I caught up, his brother was already passing two cracked leather straps to him. Peter slipped the straps over his skinny wrists and grasped the upside down T bar with each grimy hand. One mighty push from his gangly legs and he was soaring over solid ground, riding the heavily oiled metal rope with a whirr. His faded jeans flapped in the air before he bent his knees to clear the muddy water below. One of his feet skimmed the surface and brown water splashed up his legs. Even after days of rain, Jimmy always cleared the water.

My watch read five to three. Cora wasn't here yet so I waited on the old tyre hanging from an oak tree. I remembered how I'd stood on Jimmy's shoulders to loop the rope over the branch before knotting it around the tyre we'd found dumped on the beach. I pushed myself forwards and backwards and thought about the strange boy Mr O'Callaghan talked about. What did he look like? Where was he from? One of Mr Bray's nephews perhaps. All Jimmy's dad's relatives lived in England. Mr Bray stayed in Ireland to take care of his parents. He met Mrs Bray and went no further than Castletownberehaven after that.

Peter Devlin and his brother stopped playing and stared at the gap in the hedge. It was Cora. She was in jeans and looked different without her smart clothes. She waved and walked over to the tree with her hands in her jacket pocket.

"Hi."

"Hello."

"Any luck at the bike shop?"

"His bike's not there."

Cora exhaled and her shoulders dropped. I swung on the tyre and watched her look over to Peter and his brother. Peter grinned at her and grabbed the pulley again, this time giving out a 'yahoo' and an extra hard push from the platform. I was glad when his feet dragged in the mud again. Stupid show-off. Cora shook her head and turned to face me.

I looked at my fingernails and started picking a bit of loose skin from my thumb. "Mr O'Callaghan said something interesting though." I jumped off the tyre and looked at Cora's face with its eggshell white skin. I had her complete attention. Mr O'Callaghan's story came out, about Jimmy last summer with a strange boy, how they had waded into the river after a trapped salmon and how Jimmy caught the fish with his bare hands.

Cora went to the swing and sat in the tyre. She let her feet off the ground and rocked a little. "He was quite a fisherman."

"Too good a fisherman to drown."

Cora jumped from the swing. "He could've slipped, hit his head."

"There wasn't a mark on him."

"How do you know?"

I yanked the loose skin from my thumb and it bled. "It was me who found Jimmy's body, in the river, on my birthday." The words pierced the air and flew into Cora, forcing her to take a step back.

"You found him!"

Her accent sounded strong and she felt like a stranger again. I wanted to take my words back, wrap them up carefully and bury them deeper this time so they wouldn't escape.

Cora reached out and put her hand on my shoulder. "It must've been hard for you."

My head dropped and I turned away from her. Peter and his brother were gone. I went over to the pulley and sat on one of the steps. Cora followed and sat next to me.

"You don't have to say any more." Cora rubbed my back.

I sucked the blood from my thumbnail and felt it sting. "I haven't told anyone." I turned my face to her. "The newspapers said a drowned boy was found by fishermen. I was going to tell people it was me and my dad, I don't know, I couldn't." I'd carried this with me for weeks, let it embed itself into my skin like a cat of nine tails laced with razor blades. Saying I'd found him was the hardest bit, I couldn't tug at the rest of it slowly, like I did with a plaster over a healed cut, it had to come away in one go, quickly, or else the agony would be prolonged. I told Cora about my birthday, how Dad had taken me fishing after we'd seen salmon in the river. I was glad when Cora stopped rubbing my back and put her hands back in her pocket. It made it easier to talk without the distraction of how good her affection felt.

"Dad was putting bait on our fishing rods when I saw a clump of black hair caught against a rock. It looked like a dead cat so I went over to have a look." Something inside me shifted. It came up to the back of my eyes and pushed water forward. I wiped my cheek. "It was Jimmy."

Cora put her arm around my shoulder and we sat in silence on the steps. The birds carried on singing and the trees swayed in the breeze, their light rustle meant time had only stopped for us. Cora took her arm from around me and the wind separated us again. She stood and brushed the back of her jeans with her hands. We walked quietly to Cora's aunt's cottage and if only I could have reached out and grabbed her to stop her going in. I wanted to see her again, go somewhere together, dressed up, with her perhaps wearing a little perfume borrowed from her aunt, and me wearing dad's tie, after telling him I had a date. I needed to talk to Dad, to plan. I had no idea where we could go. That would take too long, it could be the end of the week before I saw Dad again.

"I want to go to Castletown after school on Monday and see if Jimmy's bike is there. Will you meet me at the bus stop after school?" The words tumbled from my mouth like marathon runners.

"I don't think my aunt will let me."

"Say you're staying late to study."

Cora looked at the ground. "I want to, I really do, if my aunt finds out I've lied to her… "

I touched Cora's arm and she looked up. "Please come."

She smiled and I loved how her whole expression changed. I didn't want her to answer me straight away, I wanted to let my eyes roam over her face and memorise every bit of it. She pushed a loose ringlet behind her ear. "Okay, I'll think of something to tell my aunt."

four

I told Mam at lunch I was going to the Bray's after school. It was risky but wherever I said I might be there was always someone who might blow my cover. Other girls surrounded Cora all day making it impossible to be near her. Now she knew about me finding Jimmy I worried in case she told anyone else my secret. It's not that I didn't like her knowing, I did, it meant there was a bond between us. Having to wait until after school until I could talk to her again was agony. She smiled at me at afternoon registration, the kind of smile that said *it's okay, don't worry.* It made me feel better. The rest of the afternoon was spent thinking about Cora, about asking her out, or buying her a gift. I imagined her face as it had been at her aunt's gate yesterday evening. When the final bell rang I rushed to the bus stop. It seemed ages before Cora arrived.

"Hi, Anthony, what's up?"

"Nothing."

"I mean how are you, silly."

I smiled. "You're wearing jeans." They were the same style as the ones she wore yesterday, except darker, newer.

"I changed in the bathroom. I hate wearing skirts." She hauled her gym bag from her shoulder and dumped it on the ground. "Jeez that's heavy."

A crowd of bustling third years pushed us towards the school bus.

"This isn't our bus," said Cora.

"I know. Let's walk to the next stop so no one sees us." I offered to carry her bag. She passed it to me laughing saying I'd change my mind as soon as I knew how heavy it was. Cora made out she was taking her gym kit home to be washed, although the sharp edges against my back told me it was full of books.

"Here, let me carry yours." Cora took my hold all. "A compromise."

There was no way a girl from Cork would've done that.

"What's Castletownbere like?"

"Dad says they've the biggest fishing fleet in southwest Ireland. It's a perfect location, sheltered from Atlantic storms by Bere Island."

"Is there a chance the fish I ate for supper last night might have come from there?"

"Maybe," I said. My thoughts moved to Jimmy catching the salmon with his bare hands. It must have been a few minutes before the bus arrived, and unzipped the comfortable silence Cora and I were lost in.

I paid the driver and let Cora sit near the window. A familiar man rang the bell for the next stop.

"Will I see your dad at the hotel tonight, Tony?" he said.

"You will," I replied.

The man looked at Cora and batted the side of his nose with his forefinger. He winked. "I'll not say I saw ye."

I scanned the other seats and there was one mother with a toddler. She held him secure whilst he stood making squiggles on the steamy window. I turned to Cora. "That was close."

"My aunt thinks I'm studying in the library before having dinner with Patty O'Driscol tonight. I told Patty to cover for me. There should be no problem."

I wondered if Cora had told Patty about our talk yesterday. The woman with the toddler rang the bell and broke my train of thought. She struggled to hold the child and balance when the bus slowed down and it was natural to give her a hand. The woman got off the bus with the baby and I looked over my shoulder as I waited to pass the pushchair down. Cora was reaching to the floor in the walkway between the seats. She picked something up, a purse. She opened it and glanced at me. I looked away too late. The mother settled the toddler into the buggy and thanked me. I nodded to the driver and he pulled off before the exit swished shut.

"Wait!" It was Cora. "Your wallet."
The bus stopped abruptly sending Cora into me. "Driver, will you open the doors please?" Cora handed the lady her purse.

"You could've kept that," I tried.

"Nah. It had her son's picture inside."

I wasn't sure if she was serious or not and felt thick for giving her a leading statement. She wiped condensation from the window with her glove and I wished the atmosphere would clear as easily as the steam on the glass had done. Cora broke the silence.

"I wasn't going to steal it, if that's what you think."

"No, I don't think that." What an idiot, I'd made a mountain out of a molehill.

"I was curious about what was inside," she said.
I found myself telling Cora about a time in Bantry with Jimmy one Saturday afternoon after going to the pictures. Jimmy and I had been to see *Quadrophenia* and were high as kites. Not because we'd passed for eighteen at the ticket office, but because for a couple of hours that afternoon we left behind our dreary lives of school, church and patchwork fields, and joined a world of music and life in England. Phil Daniels, who played Jimmy Cooper, was our hero and we hated Gordon Sumner. I was pushing my Jimmy along a Bantry street singing the chorus to *Bellboy*. Passers-by shook their heads in disgust and once in a phone box we both

doubled up in hysterics for making the adults think we were serious. I'd promised Mam I'd phone her and let her know what bus I was catching home, and I tried to stop laughing when I dug into my pocket for the coin she'd given me. Then I noticed on the shelf next to the phone there was a purse. We looked around to make sure no one could see us and I opened it. There was about five pounds in loose change, and when I un-popped the press-stud the insides were filled with notes and a credit card. If I'd been a dog I'd have barked fiercely when a knock pounded the phone-box glass. It was a man in a black leather jacket with a Derry accent. He reached out for the purse, saying it was his wife's. I handed it over and he found his manners, thanking us profusely. We bragged to each other on the bus ride home we would have kept the purse and spent the money on alcohol. That afternoon after seeing the film, it no longer felt wrong to keep a stranger's money. At confession some weeks later, I found myself mentioning it to Father Molony. He made me say half the rosary in penance, and I decided to be selective about what I'd bring to the confessional in future.

"Glad I'm not Catholic," said Cora after I'd finished telling her.

"You can't be Protestant, your dad went to the same school as mine."

Cora said her father gave up going to church when he left Ireland, and on Sundays her parents would work so she'd hang out with her friends on the air-force base. "Mom left it for me to decide if I want religion or not," she continued.

"I don't think I've ever met anyone who's not a Catholic before."

Cora giggled and jabbed me in the arm. I feigned injury and she poked me in the ribs making me laugh.

"You look a bit like Phil Daniels. Anyone ever tell you that?"

I shook my head and glowed inside. Ever since I'd since the film I'd wanted to look like Jimmy Cooper. My nose was big enough and I'd persuaded the barbers to give my dark hair a cut like his.

"Castletown!" called the driver. He looked down the bus at us in his rear view mirror and winked. I cleared my throat and stood, straightening my blazer before I shimmied into the aisle.

We moved out into the icy wind. The afternoon was fading and lit streetlights dotted the pavement. A pub door leaned open and men's voices flowed out with the smell of tobacco smoke and beer.

Cora stopped outside a clothes shop and looked in at the dummies. "See that coat? In America it would be half the price. Ireland is expensive."

We passed a record shop. "Are records cheaper too?"

"Yeah, everything is."

"It would take me weeks to save up for a record on what Mr Bray gives me."

"Let me know what you want, someone will send it from America."

"Oh, no, that's okay, thanks anyway."

Cora shrugged. What could I give her no one else could? I earned money on the farm but everything she needed could be sent from abroad.

Johnston's bike shop was up ahead. Relieved the window-shopping was over, we walked in to the sound of a ringing phone. A man in his twenties with a short back and sides left a pen on the ledger and picked up the receiver. To the left a door marked 'staff only' had a unicycle propped against its frame, the type I'd seen at a circus and not imagined existed in the real world.

"Hey look, a *Schwinn.* My dad has one of these." Cora turned to the shop assistant and waited a moment for him to put down the phone receiver. "How much is this?" she asked.

"Ahh, not for sale I'm afraid. What yer looking at there is a ninety fifties Red Phantom. Sold to me by Sean Doherty after he put his fine place up for auction; seventy acres of land no less. Brought the bike back with him from America after going out there for work. Missed the grey fields of home though he said. Came back, couldn't live here either. Half his heart's in the land of the free, the other in the Emerald Isle. He'll never settle that one."

I saw a flicker of something behind Cora's eyes and it struck me Cora might become sick of Ireland and want to return home to the States, like Sean Doherty's mirror image. A lump scraped at the pit of me.

Cora moved her attention back to the bike and ran a hand over the chipped paintwork. "It's beautiful," she crooned.

"Needs a paint and a polish, sure as the saints I'll be riding it to work."

"Have you been offered a *BMX* recently from a couple in Barley Cove?" I asked.

"Can't say I have. You're not one of those bunny hoppers are you?" The assistant winked.

I thought of Jimmy on his bike bunny hopping outside a standpipe at the Westwood playground. "My friend, Jimmy Bray, he died recently and I'm not sure what happened to his bike."

"I see, can't exactly ask the family at a time like this. We were sorry to hear of young Jimmy dying. You will send our condolences?"

"For sure," I replied.

"Sorry though, I've not seen your friend's bike. Why don't you leave your phone number with me and I can give you a ring should I happen to come across it."

Cora nodded to me and the lad pushed a pad and pen over to the customer's side. I scribbled down my number and let the assistant cast a look at it.

He kept his eyes on the page and said, "Would it not have come from England, the *BMX*?"

Cora and I flicked a glance to each other.

"Jimmy said it was a gift. It didn't occur to me to ask where it was from." And it hadn't. Where the bike had come from didn't matter. The morning Jimmy told me he'd finally got the *BMX*, the excitement he wore shone. He was proud to be the only one in Barley Cove to own the must-have bike of the year. Back then it needed work doing to it and our heads were full of how to get hold of the materials for the job.

The assistant assured me he'd be in touch if Jimmy's bike turned up. We left the shop but there was a gnawing in my head.

"Anthony, are you okay?" said Cora. She rubbed my arm bringing me back to the moment.

"I don't understand why Jimmy was secretive. The boy salmon fishing with him, not saying the bike was from England."

"Who said it did come from England? The whole craze started in California, that guy doesn't know for sure."

"The Brays probably dumped it. I bet to them it was a worthless second-hand bike. It was silly of me to think it was worth anything."

"It would have been worth *something*."

I told Cora about its condition before Jimmy and I lovingly restored it and how the bike must have come from England, as it was a couple of years old.

"Maybe they gave it away," Cora tried.

"Who to?"

Cora shrugged.

The shop assistant slid the bolts on the entrance from inside, prompting us to move out into the street. It was time for me to shut up before Cora lost patience with me. I mulled over the events since Jimmy's death as we approached the bus stop.

My mouth opened and I listened to the words tumble from me with a will of their own. "What about Tom O'Leary at Jimmy's funeral? He's keeping something quiet." I leaned against the bus shelter.

Cora took a soft looking scarf from her gym bag and wrapped it around her neck. It covered her hair making it look short. "Your dad was great the way he handled him," said Cora, defusing my mood.

"Tom always does that." I craned my neck to look for the bus. "After me and Jimmy were confirmed last year Tom got drunk at the celebration afterwards. He started calling Jimmy a little bastard. In front of the priest."

"No way!" Cora started laughing. "I'm sorry, I know it's not funny." She covered her mouth with a striped mitten.

"It's lucky the bishop had gone home."

Cora brought a second gloved hand to her mouth, I could tell by her eyes she was still laughing. I didn't mind though, not one bit.

I saw the bus coming and stuck out my hand. "We should get Tom O'Leary drunk and ask him where the bike is." The access swished open and it was the same bus driver as before. "Barley Cove please."

Cora went for the seats we'd had on the way there. She wiped the window again and undid her scarf and stuffed it back into the bag. "Anthony, let's do it!"

"What, get Tom drunk?"

"Yeah."

"I was joking."

"He knows stuff. What was it he said about it all being a sham?"

"Just drunken babble, Cora."

"I'm not so sure."

I agreed with her, and it scared me. My thoughts about what Tom O'Leary said at Jimmy's funeral were out in the open. If I could go back to having to see if Jimmy's bike was in Castletown, that it was only Jimmy's bike that was missing I could have lived with that. Left it. But there was Tom's outburst. Everyone knew he was a drunk, he talked nonsense all the time when he'd too much to drink and that was that. What about Mr O'Callaghan's story about the thrashing salmon though? I rubbed my temples with my fingers and hoped an answer would appear. I pictured Mr O'Callaghan in his shop, his grey eyes that once might have been blue. He probably saw two other people and mistook Jimmy for one of them. Perfect. The image of Tom O'Leary falling into Mrs Bray's buffet table replayed in my head.

"We need to talk to Tom."

"Yes!" Cora clapped her gloves together.

The bus reached Barley Cove and we jumped from it into the night air.

"Thanks Anthony, I enjoyed our trip … if that's the right word … I mean…"

"I enjoyed it too."

Cora looked relieved. I didn't want her to feel wrong for being happy. I was floating on her exuberance, and when I left her at the cottage gate that evening being careful not to be spotted by her aunt, I took the buoyancy she'd given me and managed to pray that night, thanking God for making Cora. Mam smiled at me when I got home, something she rarely did since Jimmy died. I caught my reflection in the hall mirror on the way to the kitchen. My face had lost its frown I had grown used to lately. I ate soda bread at the kitchen table and let the oven-warm air wrap me in sleepiness, and I wondered if Cora would listen to her radio before she fell asleep that night.

It's seven thirty and here is the news: the one hundredth and ninth UDR soldier has been found shot dead at his place of work in a timber yard in Londonderry. Twenty seven year-old...

I felt around the radio for the volume switch and turned it down. Was it Saturday yet? No, another school day.

Jimmy's face in the water ran through my head. It wasn't the first thing I thought of when I woke up, that was something. The night I found him I didn't sleep at all. I don't think Mam or Dad did either because we all had dark circles under our eyes at breakfast. Nobody spoke and we barely ate our food. The night after I slept a bit, although my sleep was disturbed, not by thoughts of Jimmy, but by dark, contorted faces. I was afraid to shut my eyes in case they appeared, and after several nights like this, I was exhausted. Mam took me to the doctor and he gave me a prescription. I started sleeping better, but the first thing that slammed into my head with the alarm was Jimmy's wet head. Now it was the second thing. Progress.

Summer Nights followed the news and I thought about John Travolta and Olivia Newton John singing in the sumptuous American sunshine. My mind flicked to the Bray's farm before autumn had called a halt to short sleeves. It was one of those gorgeous, sunshiny days; the kind I thought America had all the time, like in *Grease* and *Charlie's Angels*. Millie was in the paddock with Jimmy and I was sitting on top of the gate, sipping Mrs Bray's homemade lemonade. The windows of the farmhouse were wide open and Mrs Bray appeared from time to time to prop a mop outside or bat a rug over the clothesline. Tom O'Leary arrived in his truck with fuel for the stove. Millie's soft nose appeared next to me and I brushed the bristles on her chin, admiring her white blaze and long, dark eye lashes.

"Come over here and help your Uncle Tom, Jimmy." Tom drew out a grey hanky which must once have been white, and with it mopped his forehead.

Jimmy climbed over the paddock gate, muttering under his breath. I asked him what was wrong; he ignored me and paced to the barn with his hands plunged into his trouser pockets, the back of his head a mass of long black curls that showed a tint of red in the sun. I thought he was going to fetch a spade so I jumped from the gate to make a start with Tom. I heard Jimmy slam the barn door behind him.

"He's in for it now," said Tom. He wiped his hands down his trousers and followed Jimmy into the barn.

Millie neighed and began flitting around in the paddock, kicking up the fine powdery sand dried in the heat. Mrs Bray appeared in the farmhouse doorway. "Will you calm the horse down there, Tony? I've cleaned the house and she'll fill it with dust again, she will."

I dropped the turf and went back to the gate and into Millie's paddock. Every time I got near her she trotted away from me nervously. "She's spooked, Mrs Bray," I called. Millie moved to the centre of the paddock and swished her tail.

Mrs Bray was craning her neck. "Where's Jimmy?" she asked.

"He's in the barn with his uncle." I left Millie and made a second attempt to unload the truck.

"Will he not help Tom and be done with it?" She tutted and took a broom into the house with her.

It was left to me to unload the Bray's turf. Mam would sometimes joke my father and I would disappear when it was time to do the washing up – now I knew what she meant. Any help available when Tom arrived had scattered; even the horse didn't want to know. I hummed the tune to *Doctor Jimmy* by The Who whilst I stacked the muddy pieces into the bunker. Then I sat on Mrs Bray's step to wait for Jimmy. *Doctor Jimmy and Mister Jim.*

Tom came out of the barn and pulled a pack of tobacco from his pocket. He rolled a cigarette and lit it. The smoke hung on the hot afternoon air and Tom hacked a chesty cough. "Home with you, Tony."

There was no sign of Jimmy.

"You're going to be late!" It was Mam calling up the stairs. I eased up from my bed and went to the bathroom for a wash.

five

It was quiet at the farm that evening and Mrs Bray said it was fine just to tidy up the yard and make sure Millie was settled for the night. I led Millie from the paddock and welcomed the peace and warmth of the barn where I talked to her.

"You miss Jimmy don't ye?" I said.

Millie snorted and jerked her head up and down.

"So do I." I ran the brush over her back and down her legs to remove the dried mud of the day. I hadn't ridden her since Jimmy died. He used to ride a lot and she was used to his voice, gentle with him. Sometimes I'd ride on her back with him and we'd trot along the side of the river to the bridge down stream. We'd leave Millie to graze and go into the woods, if the weather was good. The ground was soft and dry underneath the tall pine trees. The forest was so thick the trees were bare below where no light could reach, making it easy to walk through. We'd find a small clearing and sit on the fallen brown pine needles. Sometimes Jimmy would talk about Cora and we'd hatch plans of how she might go out with him.

That was before his fourteenth birthday. Afterwards Jimmy stopped riding Millie as much. Whenever I suggested taking her out he would say he had a tummy ache, or his leg hurt or he had pins and needles. I wondered if he had growing pains, because only a few months before that my right foot hurt for weeks, and Dad put it down to growing pains. Jimmy was eight months younger than me, so it could've been happening to him too. When I suggested Jimmy go and see the doctor he said he was too scared to go to the doctor's. I offered to go with him but he said he'd just take one of his mother's pain-relief tablets and that it wasn't worth making a fuss about. I stopped asking to take Millie out.

"Poor Millie." I covered her with her coat and patted her goodnight. The sky was grey outside and the moon shone, its grey face looked worried. I tapped on the door to the farmhouse and Mrs Bray opened it, drying her hands on a tea towel.

"Come in, come in, I'll pay you some money." She left me in the living room and disappeared behind the heavy-oak kitchen door.

All the furniture in the front room was back in its place. The sympathy cards were curled slightly from the heat of the log fire and Jimmy still smiled from his picture on the mantle piece. I looked over at the table Tom O'Leary wrecked a few days ago. Its linen tablecloth had been washed and pressed and a bowl of fresh flowers placed in its centre. The cloth fell awkwardly over one of the dining room chairs; I walked over to pull it straight, a habit I'd picked up from Mam, who would nudge pictures on walls, until a spirit level could prove it was in place. I looked at my dirty hands and took care to use only the tips of my fingers. My knuckles bounced on something hard. I lifted the cloth and saw it covered seven bottles of whiskey sitting on one of the dining-room chairs. Mrs Bray must've have forgotten they were there. I listened for her footsteps; all was quiet. I picked up one of the bottles and winced when it clinked against another. I shoved it deep into an inside pocket on my coat, then left the tablecloth as it had been. *She won't miss that,* I thought.

Mrs Bray paid me and I headed for home across the fields. The whiskey flanked my leg, and once away from the farm I realised I had taken possession of something that did not belong to me. A stampede of thoughts rushed through my head like wild stallions; *Thou Shalt not Steal* led the way to a barrage of guilt. Is this how I'd have felt if I'd kept the purse in Bantry? I took the bottle from my pocket, wanting to keep it away from me at least. The path that stripped through the ploughed earth was unpredictable in the dark; I lost my footing and turned my ankle. An old wound from playing football without warming-up first seared in disapproval. I thought about leaving the bottle at the side of the field, except the deep furrows might as well have been quick sand. I wasn't about to head back for my wellies. Arriving home knee-deep in filth would arouse suspicion. I moved my concentration from the theft and negotiated the path as best I could on my throbbing ankle. Most nights I walked home from the farm in a trance, my feet falling naturally into the trodden groves I'd made over the weeks. I thought of Cora and forgot about my ankle. I needed to tell her I had the whiskey and arrange a time for us to give it to Tom O'Leary.

There was no way Mam would let me out again this evening without giving me the Spanish Inquisition. If I went to the cottage without an invitation, Cora would be questioned when I left. I reached the gate at the bottom of the field and felt around for the rusty chain that was hooped over the post. A car rounded the bend on the lane below, and I was afraid its headlights would illuminate me. I whisked the bottle to my chest and turned my back to the car, a strange position to be in on the wrong side of the gate, maybe they didn't see me. I pushed the whiskey back into my pocket and stamped my feet on the tarmac to drop the bulk of dirt from my boots.

Mam was at the kitchen table reading the paper when I got in. She pushed a chair out for me, but there was no way I could throw my coat over it without the bottle banging on its leg or bulging from the pocket. I left my coat on and went to the stairs.

"Cold?" said Mam.

"Need to nip upstairs before I forget what I was going to do."

"Shoes!"

I backtracked to the porch and left my boots on the rack. Mam looked at the paper again and I walked the stairs as normally as I could.

I surveyed my room for a suitable hiding place. Under the bed was no good – what if Mam changed the sheets? Same with a drawer – she might put my ironing away. I settled for the back of the wardrobe. I pushed my trainers aside and buried the bottle under some sweaters that lay crumpled at the back. *She'll think I'm a raving alcoholic if she finds this hidden.* It had to be soon, I couldn't risk Mam finding the bottle.

Most of the next day in class Cora's head was in a book. I thought about passing her a note, then decided against it in case it fell into the wrong hands. I managed to catch her outside the girls' toilets at break as she waited for Patty.

"What's that you're reading?"

Cora looked up from her book. "It's Shakespeare," she showed me the cover, *Macbeth.* "My parents have been posted to England and my dad has this whole British thing going on." Cora smiled when she spoke. "He sent me the book and asked me to read it. Said he'll test me on it next time he calls."

There was probably thirty seconds before Patty reappeared and although I loved hearing Cora speak, I wanted to let her know about the whiskey. "Listen," I touched Cora's elbow to move her away from the toilets. "What we talked about yesterday, getting Tom O'Leary drunk."

"Yeah, I thought about that. You're right, it is a bad idea."

"No, *you're* right, we should do it. I've got the bottle of whiskey."

Cora's mouth opened, "Where from?"

"It doesn't matter. Can you meet me after school?"

"I'm not sure, Anthony." Cora stopped. "I can't risk getting into trouble."

"Say you'll meet me."

"Maybe."

"Ready?" It was Patty. She looked at me suspiciously and then at Cora.

I kept my eyes on Cora for as long as possible, hoping she'd nod her head or mouth the word 'okay'. Instead she turned to Patty and spoke hurriedly to her. Patty listened and giggled. I walked away, hurt a little that they might be laughing at me, thankful at least, she'd distracted Patty.

I couldn't stop thinking about Tom O'Leary all afternoon. During English I looked out of the window at the Home Economics group downstairs in the next building. My thoughts drifted as I watched them shake white flour onto their rolling pins and stretch damp pastry.

Jimmy told me nothing about what happened that hot day when Tom followed him into the barn. I asked him afterwards and he said he didn't want to talk about it. Things were becoming a little strained by then so I didn't push it. I'd wondered whether Jimmy was going off our friendship, because he'd started to make excuses for not coming out. By last October I was spending more and more time in my room alone. Mam and Dad thought it was great when the teachers gushed praise about my homework. I wondered if the boy Mr O'Callaghan saw Jimmy with was the reason my best friend stopped hanging round with me. It made sense in a way, if Jimmy had found a new friend. The friend wasn't at our school though. I wondered whether to ask Mrs Bray about him. She might start asking me why I wanted to know, and with a bottle of her whiskey in my wardrobe the last thing I wanted to do was draw attention to myself.

"Tony, read the beginning of chapter five out loud, please," said the teacher.

I left the bakers with their pastry and opened my textbook.

Cora was still with Patty after the last bell. I pretended to search in my bag for something until Cora waved goodbye to her friend. I zipped my bag and ran up beside Cora.

"Cora, can we talk?"

"What's the matter, Anthony?"

"I've been remembering some stuff about Jimmy from last summer."

"You have? I'll walk back with you." Cora struggled with her art folder as she tried to carry her book bag with one hand.

"Here, let me help you."

Cora smiled and handed over the heavy bag. "Thanks Anthony."

I carried her bag on my spare shoulder, full of books with words she would have looked at that day. I might as well have left my own books at home; I'd read one or two paragraphs at most. I was glad for the work I'd done last October as Jimmy slowly drifted away from me. Since his death I'd only been capable of producing the bare minimum. I wanted to give something my all, not my schoolwork, finding out what was hiding in the dark corners between the Brays and the O'Learys.

"Are you going to the Brays this evening?" asked Cora.

"No, I don't need to go for a couple of days, Mrs Bray paid me last night."

"Is that how you got the whiskey?"

"Not exactly."

"Anthony, I don't think I can visit Tom with you, I'll get into serious trouble if I do."

"Cora, it will be fine."

Cora stopped walking. "Sorry, Anthony, the answer's no."

"I stole for you!" I had to turn around and leave then. It was such a stupid thing to say.

By March, the biting winter had retreated, leaving a damp, woody smell that saturated the early-spring air. The stark hedgerow looked as if it would poke out small shoots at any moment, and the first green leaves of the potatoes were visible above ground, caterpillar bitten already. I'd left a sweater draped over Millie's stall being too sticky to carry it home with me. I relished the light evenings that barred the dark stallions from my mind as I trod the pathway from the farm down to the lane where Cora lived. Every evening I'd glance in the direction of her cottage to see if I could catch a glimpse of her. Tonight was the first evening this year that the light over her porch was out.

The stile that led to the field between my house and Cora's cottage was slimy. No cattle grazed here, and hadn't since I was a young boy. The O'Leary's owned this piece of land, as well as the fields directly around their farms. This one was grown over and would be thick with brambles by the end of summer. A waste, my father said, after he asked Mr O'Leary Senior if we could buy the plot. The O'Leary's would never sell. Most other farmers in the area rented their land from them, keeping what was left after lambing and harvest for themselves. Dad wanted to buy, not rent. What started as an idea to keep chickens, turned into a plan of building our own house. We had farmed once though, the Barbers, in the days of my grandfather and beyond. Dad's brother still lived in the ramshackle farmhouse they'd been raised in, on the far side of Adrigole. When my grandfather died our fields were sold on to the neighbour, Chris Dee, who agreed to let the sons keep and live in their family home. My uncle and father helped Chris Dee farm and made a decent enough living. As soon as the hotel was built in Barley Cove though, Dad said he saw a life away from the cold fields of Cork and began his life as the local handyman.

I let my thoughts sail to planning our visit to see Jimmy's Uncle Tom. Throughout the dreary winter months Cora had ignored me and I made no effort to speak to her. I was angry that she wouldn't listen to me about the memories I'd unearthed about Jimmy, memories that made no sense to me, but may have done to her. After half term, our form tutor rearranged the class seating plan, and I was moved next to Cora.

She smiled as I dropped my bag under my new desk, and said, "I know there's no other way to find out more about Jimmy's death without talking to Tom O'Leary."

We were friends again.

At first break we sat together in the playground and made plans to visit Tom and trip him up. We both knew this was not something that would happen over a polite cup of tea. Tom's continuous scowl left no invitation to approach. There was one thing Tom would never said no to though – a drink.

No one was in when I arrived home at five thirty. I rummaged through the kitchen drawer and tightly balled plastic bags leapt onto the floor and seemed to multiply like *Tribbles* on *The Star Ship Enterprise.* I wanted something thick enough to hide the bottle I would be carrying; these were too thin. Where were all the glossy bags that Christmas presents were brought home in? I stuffed the *Tribbles* back into the drawer and decided my school bag would have to do. I went into the living room and flicked on the television, falling into Dad's chair. The brown dralon was worn on the arms where his elbows sat when he read the paper. I jumped up and went to the front letterbox. The evening paper lay on the mat. I brought it into the living room and plopped it onto the teak coffee table. I curled up in the chair again and half watched cartoons that marked the end of children's TV. I glanced up at the crucifix hanging over Mam's sideboard. The palm tucked behind the cross drooped lazily around Jesus' head. I helped make the palm crosses one year, before I moved to senior school. I bent forward and peeled two strips of paper from the evening paper, holding one piece vertically in my left hand, I crossed the second piece over it and then heard the back door bang.

"It's only me," called Mam.

I crumpled the strips of paper and tossed them into the waste-paper basket. Dad's paper looked wounded on the coffee table and I hoped he would think it was Mam who had torn away at the front page in search of something to reach into the stove with and light the fire. I skidded into the kitchen on socked feet.

Mam dropped two bulging polythene bags onto the kitchen table and pulled off her beige mac. "It's mild out there," she said. She walked to the sink and washed her hands.

I peeked inside the carriers feeling as if I hadn't been fed for a week. Mam walked over and slapped my hand.

"Out," she said.

"What time's tea, Mammy?"

"Six as usual. Have you done your homework?"

"I have. Any crisps?" I asked.

"There's some in the larder, don't spoil your tea."

I grabbed the crisps and stuffed a couple more bags under my jumper, in case Cora had not eaten.

The gate to the cottage was open, which meant Cora's Aunt Peg was out. I checked to make sure no one was looking and made my way down the garden path to the knotted wooden entrance with its wrought iron knocker. I tapped three times. Cora appeared briefly at a front window and then dodged back before I could acknowledge her. The letterbox rattled before the wooden hunk creaked open to nudge and bounce back from a doorstop. Cora was in black again. I thought back to Jimmy's funeral, the first time we spoke.

"Ready?" I asked.

"As I'll ever be."

She pulled the entrance behind her and we walked up the path onto the road. Tom's was a fifteen-minute walk. It was six-thirty and we were both to be in by nine. We'd a good chance of getting him drunk in that time, and if not we'd be late home. I thought about the consequences of not arriving home in time. Mam would probably give me an hour before she started asking the neighbours if anyone had seen me. It depended on whether Dad was home or not. If he was, he would tell her not to worry and I'd have a little more leeway. Also, there was Cora to consider. Her aunt sounded strict and I didn't want Cora to be given a curfew. There was no clue at that point that a curfew would have been welcomed rather than what eventually transpired. We walked quickly and silently, using each spare moment to pick up the pace. It was unusual to walk in this direction with a school bag, with Tom's being the last house in the village before the coastline. Thankfully we only saw one or two cars, filled with strangers passing through, heading for Bantry for an evening out or to see relatives. To our left Hungry Hill growled when we stepped on its toes, threatening to gobble us up if we slackened our speed. Tom's house came into view, its white masonry cracked and broken. In front of a low wall a cloudy-eyed collie barked half-heartedly. It was Pup, and he was as blind as a bat. Cora ran her hand over his head and his tail lifted lazily in an attempt wag. Although Tom's house was wide open, this was no guarantee he'd be in. Inside was dark and all that could be seen was last year's fly bait hanging crookedly from the ceiling. A rasping cough told me Tom was home.

"Pup!" he shouted. I heard his feet scuff the stone floor. He appeared in braced trousers, his head bald without his cap.

"Yes?"

"Present from Mr Bray, sir." I unzipped my bag and offered the Irish whiskey.

Tom swiped it and read the label. His eyebrows raised and a smile crept to his lips. "Couldn't have come at a better time."

He curled a hand inviting us in. I looked at Cora and felt a jolt of excitement when we crossed the threshold. My eyes slowly adjusted to the dark. Tom fell back into an armchair and cracked the lid of the bottle open. On a small table next to him, a glass stood, translucent, aged and in good need of a wash. He tipped the drink into it and swallowed in one. Tom licked his lips and I glanced around the room. It was barely furnished for one, in the far corner an oak dresser stood adorned with photographs of Jimmy and Mrs Bray. Tom caught me looking.

"'Tis Jimmy and his Ma," he said.

Only Jimmy and his Ma, I thought.

He poured another glass and I looked nervously at Cora. We weren't invited to sit down, there was nowhere to perch anyway. Cora signalled to the exit with her eyes.

"We only came to drop the whiskey off," I croaked.

"Go on, off with ye!" said Tom leaning forward in his chair. His cordial mood fading fast with each sip. Cora and I turned to leave and Pup moved out of the way.

"Say thank you to yer man at the farm," called Tom.

We walked gently to his gate and turned left towards home in case he was watching us. The plan was to wait on the beach until Tom passed out. Several metres from Tom's a locked wooden gate guarded a field of sheep and lambs. I climbed over first sending a cluster of lambs scrambling, bleating in search of their mothers.

"Ssh!" Pup may have been blind, he wasn't deaf. I doubted Tom was drunk enough yet to not respond to his sheep dog's concern.

Cora waited until the young sheep were settled and pushed herself up before swinging a slender limb over the other side of the gate. I followed the shape of her calf up to her thigh.

"Quit staring!"

I averted my gaze and gave in to a warm flush of embarrassment. "Not bad for a girl," I said, in an attempted cover-up.

Cora swiped my shoulder and shook her head before ploughing on and I ran a little to catch up with her.

The ewes stood foursquare and eyed us warily on the trodden path towards the seashore. It was six forty-five and I guessed it would take Tom at least an hour to pass out. That would make it seven forty-five when we could go back to his house. I'd wait all night if need be, when would we have another opportunity of coming across a spare bottle of whiskey *and* getting Tom to drink it straight away? It had to be tonight we searched Tom's house.

Cora and I trailed through a cow field and made it to the pebbly shore. Darkened stones the waves could no longer reach meant high tide had passed. We sat on the dry band and Cora picked fragments of shell and arranged them in patterns on her palm.

"It's hard to believe these were once a creature's home," she said.

I looked out to sea and thought about my father, how his working all hours at the hotel was breaking off chunks from the Barber home.

"I'm glad we're out of there," said Cora.

I turned to her. "You mean Tom's?"

"Yeah, where else?"

"Sorry, I was thinking about my father." I looked into Cora's hand at a mosaic of seashells. My father was the flinty matchstick-shaped one, and Jimmy the white ridged, neither fitting with any of the broken pieces. "Do you think to God they make a whole?" I asked, pointing to Cora's collection.

"I think they're broken pieces of shell on a beach," and she tossed them skyward, letting them disappear between the pebbles when they landed.

"What is it you think Tom's hiding?"

"I dunno," said Cora.

"Someone must know what happened to Jimmy. If there's something to know, it means we can find out what it is."

"Hey, this sea air's getting to you isn't it? What do you say we go back to Tom's, see if the old brute's passed out yet?"

"For sure," I said, standing.

I held out a hand for Cora. She reached up and stood, barely needing my hand to steady her. "You know, somewhere the other bits of those shells exist," she said. The wind dragged her hair across her face, like a veil forbidding her to utter another word.

We trudged back across the field in silence as the light dimmed. I was glad I'd brought my school bag along and reached into the front pocket for a small black rubber torch. I pointed it against the gate to check it was working and its beam picked out one of the rotting bars. Cora climbed over and I hurled my backpack before me. My heart-rate was knocking at the thought of searching Tom's.

I switched off the torch near the road. Birds were singing evensong and an occasional lamb's bleat rose from the field. Tom's house stood in darkness against the cloudy sky. Pup was nowhere to be seen and the front was still open. We stood at the gate for a few moments listening for any sign of life inside. Cora moved to one side to stand guard and I walked to the outhouse with the flashlight as a weapon. A look through one of the small windows showed me nothing. I wiped the pane then jumped back and clutched my chest when two shiny-eyes appeared. I clicked on the torch and a black cat jumped from a stall. The sound of its feet rustled in the hay and I wondered if the herd were milked or left fit-to-burst with heavy udders. The outhouse was open and I moved on inside in case Tom was passed out in there. Cobwebs brushed my face and gripped my hair. Sacks of grain were stacked haphazardly against the outside wall, one spilling onto the barn floor where mice had dined. In the cool evening air the cow-stalls smelled green and sickly. There was no sign of Tom.

"He's not in there," I said to Cora, on my return.

"Leaves one thing for it."

Blue light reflected from her left cheek. If she didn't move, remained there until tomorrow, I could watch her through the night, a time we'd yet to spend together. Cora's hand touched my arm and for a moment I thought she was going to kiss me. I parted my lips, terrified I wouldn't know what to do. She found my hand and took the torch from me. I was relieved and disappointed at the same time. She moved away and I brought my attention back to Tom, his shrine to Jimmy and Jimmy's mother, Tom's sister.

Cora took the lead down the short path. She knocked delicately and shouted 'hello'. No answer. We stepped inside, the embers in the fireplace were the only sign of life.

"He must be upstairs asleep," I said. "You search the dresser with the torch. I'll start in that cupboard under the stairs."

"Okay."

There was a light cord under the stairs and I tugged it on. Inside, rows of shelves were cluttered with old biscuit tins, rusty cans with no labels and empty whiskey bottles, some plugged with candles. A lumpy sack slouched in a corner, next to it an empty mouse trap. Strewn across everything were cobwebs.

"This hasn't been touched in years." I pulled the light cord and found my way to Cora.

"Look at this," she said, handing me a piece of clear tubing.

"What is it?"

"Some sort of medical apparatus I'd say."

"Looks like evidence to me." I shoved it into my pocket. "Anything else?"

"Apart from cutlery, headache pills."

"Let's try the kitchen."

Cora shone the torch towards the kitchen and we went in. There was a roll of barking and the click clack of claws on the wooden floor. Cora found the dog with the torch and Pup launched himself at her with his menacing cloudy eyes and threatening teeth.

"Pup, off!" I grabbed his collar and Cora shrieked when she hit the floor, sending the torch rolling.

Pup's tail wagged and he licked my hand. I let go of his collar and he went to Cora and licked her face.

"Away you stupid animal." Cora rubbed her back. "I'm hurt," she said. "I landed on the base of my spine."

A mushroom of concern grew inside me and I put my arms around her. Her body jerked a little and I realised she was crying. I held her until she leaned back, and a glint of light caught a tear on her cheek. I wiped it softly with my thumb, her skin thin and smooth. The smile came back and she gave a little laugh before dragging the sleeve of her cardigan along her face.

"Will I be taking you home?" I said.

"No, I'm okay. Help me up." She held onto my arm and rose slowly from the ground. "Jesus, that hurt. You!" she said, pointing at Pup.

The dog turned tail and clicked along the floor back into the kitchen. I picked up the torch, took Cora's hand and followed him. I found the dog sitting upright next to a floored Tom, face down, the empty bottle of whiskey not far from his grasp. The cold of the wall crept along my bones as I searched for a light switch. On went the light, I saw nothing of the room. Not the stove, the larder or the potted herbs on the windowsill. All I saw was the pool of blood around Tom's head. Cora's breath caught in the back of her throat and she brought a shaking hand to her mouth.

"What the…" A man's voice.

We turned sharply and in the doorway behind us, in black shirt and jacket, a strip of white at his throat, stood Father Molony.

six

"This way," I said hurriedly, and grabbed Cora's hand. What made me do it I don't know, fear, instinct, stupidity? I jumped over Tom, and Cora tripped over him whilst I unlatched the grimy back-door handle. A deep black silhouette of trees pressed against a mottled sky.

"Careful," I whispered to Cora.

Outside thistles tugged at my trousers like hands trying to me pull me back.

"Shit! My jeans." said Cora.

"Don't worry about them," I replied, and gave her hand a small yank to move her forward.

The ground was uneven and I had no idea whether the soft patches were mole holes or cow pats. My weak ankle twisted and I gasped when a shot of pain flew up my leg.

"You okay?"

"I'm fine." I glanced over my shoulder and saw an overweight figure in Tom's doorway. Then the kitchen light went out.

"Who's out there?" came a gruff voice.

There was a brush of shoes against the scrub and the heavy breath of a man straining to quicken his pace.

We ran towards the beach. The pebbles would be hard to run on but we would be faster than the man chasing us.

Cora started lagging behind and I yanked her again. "Come on!"

"Anthony, my hip, I don't think I can."

"You have to. He's coming. Please." I tugged at her arm again but this time she resisted.

"I'm in pain." There was fear in her voice and I had to stop.

"You go," she said.

"No. Not without you."

"Who's there?" said the darkness.

"I'm sorry," said Cora.

I wrapped my arm around her shoulder and her wet cheek rested in my neck. "It's okay," I whispered. "I'm sorry for dragging you out here."

"I see you, don't move!" It was Father Molony.

How would I explain this? Should I confess that we believed Tom O'Leary murdered Jimmy Bray, that we got Tom drunk so we could search his house for clues? What else could I say? Tom was lying on his kitchen floor with his head bashed in.

"Please Father, can we get a doctor?"

"Tony Barber, is that you? What are you doing out here in the dark?"

"It's a long story, Father. Can you help me get my friend inside, she's hurt."

"I'm sorry, sir," said Cora.

"It's all right, child." Molony looked into Cora's face. "What is it?"

Cora's sobs escaped as the priest listened to her say where she was hurt. We helped her back to Tom O'Leary's kitchen where Father Molony switched on the light. Tom's blood was now tracked in footprints to the back. I scrunched my eyelids tightly shut and dug my hand into my pocket. The plastic tube was smooth, coiled and safe.

"Are you going to tell me what happened before I call the Garda?"

"The front door was open, Father, and no light on. We came in and found him on the floor there. Then we heard someone coming and thought you were the burglar. That's why we ran away."

Father Molony looked over at Cora. "You're Peggie Sheehan's niece are you not?"

"Yes, sir."

Call him Father, I willed, but Cora knew no different.

"So what were the pair of you doing out here?"

"I wanted to show Cora the walk from here to the beach, Father."

"Anthony noticed Tom's front door wide open, with all the lights out. We came through to check Tom was okay," said Cora. "When Pup wasn't outside we knew something was wrong, didn't we, Anthony?"

I nodded.

"You've been along here before then have ye?" asked Father Molony.

"No, but Anthony told me Pup always waits outside the front of the house."

Father Molony looked over at the empty whiskey bottle again. "*Powers*. Isn't that what we were drinking at Jimmy Bray's funeral?"

"I don't know, Father," I said.

"No, I suppose you wouldn't. I came to see Tom about five o'clock. He'd just about finished a bottle of whiskey. Not that one though," he said, pointing to the empty bottle of *Powers* Cora and I had given Tom. "I check on him every evening. God knows he's got steadily worse with the drink since his brother Dominic moved onto the Hill. They'll not serve him in the The Bull anymore, not after what happened."

There was a pause and Cora and I exchanged glances.

Molony continued. "How he got hold of a bottle of Powers I don't know. The Lord knows Tom's never any money." He squatted next to Tom. "He must've fallen down drunk and hit his head." The priest felt

Tom's neck. He moved his fingers two or three times and I guessed he was looking for a pulse. Then he closed his eyes, shook his head solemnly and crossed himself.

Walking back to the village Cora and I remained silent and let Father Molony rehash the details of what the police and ambulance crew had done. Cora's Aunt Peggie would be in when we reached her cottage and I had no idea where Cora said she had been. Cora looked at me anxiously from time to time and we both knew that we were in serious trouble. There was a light on in the front room when Father Molony pushed open Cora's gate. Cora walked through and I waited, hoping just the two of them would go in.

"You too, Tony," said the priest.

Cora lead and I heard her aunt call her name. She appeared in the hallway and surveyed the priest and me with surprise.

"Is everything all right, Father?"

"No there's been a terrible accident, Peggie. It's Tom O'Leary, young Tony and Cora here found him dead tonight in his house."

"Begod, Cora. What on earth …?"

"We thought Tom had been burgled and went in to investigate."

"Tom fell and hit his head, Peggie. 'Tis a terrible tragedy."

"Poor Tom. I can't take it in," said Cora's aunt, and she stumbled backwards into the hallway chair.

"Would you like a drink of water, Aunty?" said Cora.

"Yes please."

Cora disappeared into the kitchen and Peggie Sheehan looked me up and down. "What were you doing with my niece, Tony Barber?"

"Nothing!"

"Seems they were having an evening stroll, Peggie. Tom would have been there until tomorrow if they hadn't called in."

"Yes, Father. Sorry Father, 'tis a shock so it is."

"Ah, we're all feeling it, Peggie."

Cora returned with the water and the priest urged me to go home. Leaving the three in the cottage I left quietly, glad to be dismissed. Father Molony had convinced Peggie Sheehan that her niece was a heroine for discovering Tom's body. Something didn't make sense though; the priest had said Tom wouldn't have been found until tomorrow if Cora and I hadn't gone into his house. Surely Tom would have been found by the priest. An uncomfortable thought nagged in my head, that perhaps Tom hadn't fallen and hit his head, but that someone had bashed it in. The thought was crazy, this was Barley Cove, people weren't murdered. Did I really believe Jimmy was murdered? Maybe not, but there was no way he'd drowned in that river, just as there was no way a professional drunk like Tom O'Leary had smashed his own head in.

Thankfully my parents were out when I arrived home. In my room I took the rubber tubing from my pocket and sat down with it in my hands. It would have been outside in the shed if it was for use on Tom's herd, besides, it was too clean. I'd seen something similar on my grandfather before he passed away, a catheter I think they'd called it. It took urine from his bladder into a bag when he was too weak to make it to the toilet. This tube was narrow enough to be used on a human. When Tom was found dead this evening, his pullover had risen over his waist. There was no tubing, no bag.

"Tony!" called Mam up the stairs, "You in?"

I shoved the instrument under the mattress. "Yes, Mam!" Time to tell her what we'd told the priest.

I woke early the next day, thinking of Tom O'Leary face down in a pool of blood. The green digital numbers of the radio alarm read 06:10. The house was silent but I couldn't get back to sleep. Cora's parents would soon find out about last night's fatality. I swept back the covers and braced the chill air, then went silently to the bathroom for a wash.

The lane was quiet apart from the odd bird song. I'd been waiting thirty minutes, my hands dug deep into my coat for warmth, staring at what seemed like a fortress, until it opened, and Cora emerged, her ringlets loose over her shoulders. I ducked behind a bush in case her Aunt Peggie waved her off. Cora spotted me and glanced to the cottage window before looking back at me with a sombre face.

"Anthony, what are you doing here?"

"I had to speak to you, Cora. Last night your aunt seemed so shocked."

"She gave me the third degree after you left. She's pretty mad that I was out with you last night."

Cora looked at the ground and I sensed there was a lot more that her aunt had said about me. Ever since I can remember there had been an unspoken dislike between my family and Peggie Sheehan. Mam said it was because Peggie was a snob and that she looked down her nose at us. I couldn't imagine Peggie being nice to anyone, not even her own niece.

"My aunt's phoning my parents today about us being found with Tom's dead body."

Great. Since leaving Cora last night I'd had a feeling like a sleeping maggot in my gut. Now it was wriggling fiercely. Cora's parents had not really existed for me before. That her Aunt Peggie was contacting them, about Cora, brought them starkly to life. There would be trouble, the kind that Cora didn't deserve.

We walked to school in silence, each lost in our own private thoughts.

The teachers' words washed over me. Every time I looked at the clock only ten minutes or so had passed. I longed to be with Cora, to chatter and forget my thoughts.

At the final bell I found Cora alone.

"How's your hip today?" I asked, sorry that I had forgotten to check this morning.

"It's sore. I rubbed some 'Deep Heat' on it before bed. I'm not sure if the smell of it kept me awake or just the shock of last night. It must have been four before I got to sleep."

"I didn't sleep much either. All the stuff we saw at Tom's was rolling round in my head trying to piece itself together. I need to find out what that tubing's used for. There might be other stuff there, Cora. I want to go back to Tom's alone. I can't involve you in this anymore."

Cora smiled, as if relieved. I'd expected her to protest, but her eyes were sunken, their usual spirit gone.

"I'm not looking forward to going home this evening," she said.

"Would you like to go to the playground at Westwood with me first?"

"Yeah, but being late will only makes things worse. I'd better go."

We walked back and at the cottage gate Cora kissed

me on the cheek. It was the balm I needed. For her to risk her aunt seeing us together again, let alone kissing me, meant she must have been serious about me.

Mam was teasing her hair in the kitchen mirror when I arrived home. "Tony, are you okay?"

"Yes thanks, Mam."

"Good. I'm going over to Beth's. She's upset about Tom's accident."

It was no accident, I thought.

"I've made your dinner and it's in the oven."

"Thanks, Mam."

"Dad's at the hotel till late, but I'll be home before bedtime." She put down the comb and gave me a kiss on the cheek.

"Beth was away from work today with the shock of it all so I'm taking her a flask of chicken broth to get her on the mend."

"Okay, Mam."

"I feel bad leaving you after what you've been through."

"Mam I'll be fine."

"There's my brave boy." She pinched my cheek, grabbed the flask and dropped it into a carrier bag. "Remember to switch off the oven, and make sure you do your homework before you watch television." Then she was gone.

The silence of the house hit me and my head flooded with Tom O'Leary's drunken face, the broken capillaries on his nose, the smell of warm whiskey on his breath and the dark pool of blood. I filled a glass with water and drank. Two glasses later I drew the kitchen curtains, shutting out twilight along with the world.

The telephone sat on the directory in the front room. If only I could ring Cora, find out what her parents had said, but her aunt had no phone line. I turned up the gas fire and put my hands on the guard to warm.

Cora would know what her parents had said by now. I supposed there would be a funeral for Tom. Would they come to that? Would Cora introduce me to them? The aroma of food ready to be eaten caught my senses. I forgot to duck when opening the oven and was hit with a hot whoosh that made my eyes sting.

The chicken and potatoes were soaked in gravy that spilled from the plate as I moved it to the table. I ate without pause and then cleaned up.

Pulling on my parka and shoes, I clicked off the light and left. The wind flapped through my coat and ate into my face and neck. Daytime was warm enough to be without scarf and gloves, but the evening air still nipped. Most kitchen lights were on along the row that adjoined our house. Mrs Hoben looked into the bowl whilst washing dishes with her sleeves pushed up. I dropped my head and cleared the last house before coming round to the front into the road. A man on a bicycle rang his bell and I waved to Mrs Hoben's husband. At least if Mam came home early someone could tell her what time I'd gone out.

I climbed over the stile and walked across the field that separated me from Cora's quiet lane. As the night drew in, the amber glow from Peggie Sheehan's cottage pulled me towards it. An oil-lamp flickered in the leaded window and I ducked behind a bush, watching until Cora's aunt drew the curtains. Slowly I pulled up the latch on the gate and sneaked along the hedging to the back of the cottage. There was a downstairs window in darkness and slightly above it, a room with a light on. Cora had said she had an annex room, three or four steps up from the ground floor. It was too high for me to knock at the window but a sturdy oak stood several metres from her room. I hoisted myself up on some of its pruned branches and imagined Jimmy helping me as he'd done so many times.

Nestled in the branches I could see Cora, sitting at a desk with her head down. How could she concentrate on homework at a time like this? Didn't she care? Maybe that's why she was so much cleverer than me, even in a time of crisis she could study.

I'd brought nothing up the tree with me to throw at the window so I tried waving to see if the movement might catch her eye. Then her bedroom door opened and Cora put what she was writing hastily into a desk drawer. Her aunt came through, talked for a while and then left. Cora looked out towards the tree and I waved wildly. It worked; Cora checked over her shoulder and then mouthed the word 'wait'. She went over to the door and listened at it for a second, then took the chair from her desk and wedged it beneath the handle. Then she opened the window and climbed onto the ledge, signalling for me to stand underneath and catch her. I jumped from the branches onto the soft ground beneath and let her stand on my shoulders before lowering her down. She hugged me tightly. Her hair smelled like coconut.

"Anthony, my aunt spoke to my parents this afternoon, they're sending me to England to stay with my cousin."

"No," I said, and squeezed her tighter.

"It's true," she said into my coat.

"When?" I pulled away so I could see her face.

"As soon as the ferry's booked."

"Why are they sending you away?"

"Because they think I'm bad and that my cousins will be a good influence."

"You're not bad, Cora."

She turned to face her bedroom window, and the

light illuminated her profile, a perfect line, leaving me.

My words hurried then, as if she could be gone at any moment. "Thinking that something good could come out of stealing Mrs Bray's whiskey, giving it to Tom, that was stupid. If I hadn't stolen the whiskey, convinced you to come with me to Tom's …"

Cora faced me in the dim light. "Anthony, I'm not some irritating little girl who does what everyone says. So you messed up, but I made up my own mind about joining you. I hate it, hate it that I'm being sent away, but you know what? The reason I was sent to Ireland in the first place is because I couldn't keep my pilfering hands away from the Christmas money jar."

"What do you mean?"

"In your world I'm a thief, a sinner, and I don't feel bad about it. I'm not going to hell because I moved the universe's stuff around a bit. Everything on this earth belongs to us all anyway. It's not your fault I have to go, okay? It's my a'hole parents who are to blame." Cora folded her arms. "They have no idea how much this is going to cost them in therapy."

I smiled. Her eyes met mine and she smiled too. Whatever she'd done in her past didn't change anything, I still loved her. She was leaving but it would be okay. It had to be. I could tell myself that then, as she stood, metres from me, her magic floating around her like dust swimming in sunlight. Everything would turn out all right if I just believed. I reached my arms out and Cora leaned her head on my chest, and we stood under the tree, holding each other whilst the branches rustled. She shivered and I opened my coat, wrapping it around her to give her my warmth. We swayed from side to side a little, rocking each other. If time had only stopped and replayed again and again, locking us both in that moment, never to be parted.

"I was writing you a letter," said Cora under my chin. "In case my aunt took me straight to the ferry point tomorrow."

A letter, what did it say? Perhaps it said she loved me. I squeezed her a little tighter then it hit me – a twister of pain from my heart to my mouth.

"England. I don't want you to go!"

"I don't *want* to go."

If I thought any more about her leaving, I'd collapse. My arms dropped from around Cora, and my fists clenched. I turned and struck out, smacking the tree trunk with my bare knuckles. Hot pain jolted up my arm and I shook my hand out.

"Anthony, what are you doing?" Cora walked up behind me and took my shoulder.

Her face was lined with concern but all I could feel was rage. I had to leave, get away right then, before I yelled and brought Cora's aunt from the house. My mouth opened to say something, I'm sorry, goodbye, I love you, but no words came out. Instead I brushed past Cora, along the side of the cottage, ignoring her calls. My walk changed to a jog, a run, heading for the field to get back to my house. Tears of anger streaked my cheeks. It was as if the bottom of me would fall out if I didn't run, and keep running, passed the stile that led to the short-route home, passed the corner that turned left to my house. I ran, cupping my damaged hand until there were no lights, no sound of traffic or people – only animal noises and the unsettled wind. Then I wailed into the darkness, until I creased to the ground, and I lay there, until nothing else would come out.

It was ten-thirty when I reached home. Mam and Dad were at the kitchen table, spoiling my attempt to sneak in quietly. Mam stood and walked over to me, rubbed my arm and said:

"Tony, you look terrible."

"You're late son!"

"Leave it will ye?" said Mam to my father. He got up and went into the living room.

Mam looked to me. "We were worried sick. Mrs Hoben said you went out after tea. Where have you been?"

My voice was raspy. "Cora's being sent to England."

"Oh, Tony. Sending Cora away is cruel on her and you. You've a loving family here, Tony, make no mistake."

It simply hurt too much to hear the words 'Cora' and 'away' together. "Mammy, I don't know what I'm going to do."

Mam put her arms around me, her tiny frame lost against my body. The last time we cuddled she'd enveloped me. My mother made tea and buttered fresh soda bread, then sat with me at the kitchen table, her hand over mine.

"Do you want to tell me the real reason you and Cora were found at Tom O'Leary's?"

"Jimmy didn't drown, Mam."

"Tom didn't kill him."

The bread was sticking in my chest. "Do you know something?"

"Tom O'Leary was many things but he wasn't a murderer."

"You know something, Mam, tell me."

"Your father doesn't know what's got into you."

"Don't change the subject. Mam, tell me what you know."

"Jimmy drowned, that's all I know."

"Liar!"

"Get to your room, Tony Barber. That's no way to

speak to your mammy."

I pushed my plate away and went upstairs.

My bed squeaked as I fell backwards onto it. I stared into the moonlight that glinted over my *Quadrophenia* poster. Jimmy Cooper was standing in an alley without Steph. Cora was right, I did look like him. Cooper lost Steph like I'd lost Cora. He took his scooter over the cliff – his only way out.

Where are you Jimmy Bray? Does God have you, purgatory or the devil? Jimmy wouldn't have shut me out if he could have told me what was wrong. Someone must have done something to him, sworn him to secrecy, like evil does.

I pulled the curtains shut so that the room was in darkness and I couldn't see myself reflecting back from the poster anymore. Mam knew something, I was sure of it. She'd been losing weight since Jimmy's death as if she was pining too. Her and Dad were rarely together now. Before Jimmy died I'd catch them having a cuddle in the kitchen or Dad patting her bottom. He'd pick her flowers on the way home from work and she'd pretend to disapprove but then always put them in her prettiest vase.

I'd never given Cora flowers. When I held her earlier in her garden she'd given me butterflies. I wondered if she felt the same. She would probably adjust to our separation far quicker than I would. Cora had moved around so much that I wondered if she ever really grew attached to anyone.

Jimmy's death had changed everything.

I found my way to Cora's the next morning. It was the most important task I'd ever had to do, to catch her before she left. After the way it ended last night I was terrified that she would think of me as a lunatic.

Perhaps she wouldn't be far wrong. Her aunt was bound to try and head me off at the pass, but that didn't matter, I had to say goodbye.

The front of the cottage was open and a man I didn't know was dropping a suitcase into the boot of a shiny green Hillman. I glimpsed Cora inside the cottage with her coat on and butterflies fluttered through my ribs. I called her name and she looked over her shoulder then glanced toward a back room before approaching me, her eyes downcast.

"Cora I'm so sorry I left you alone last night."

She hugged me with the same intensity and I loved her for it.

"I thought I was going to go without seeing you." Her voice was shaky and sounded close to tears. She pulled back slightly and then reached into her pocket. "Here's the letter I was writing you."

The envelope was crumpled as if she'd slept with it under her pillow, and I wanted to tear it open right then, but our last moments were precious.

"I'll write again when I get there. Get to the post early every morning to make sure your parents don't hide my letters."

We hugged again, squeezing each other tightly. My breath caught on my throat. "I love you," I said quietly into her neck.

"I love you too," she said, through tears.

Cora snuffled and I gave her a tissue. I noticed her aunt standing in the porchway with her arms crossed. She shook her head and called to her niece.

Cora wiped her nose. "I have to go." She dropped her head again and I held her.

"Bye, Anthony."

I let her go, and thought about a stupid saying that I'd heard: if you love someone set them free, and if they're yours they'll come back.

Cora turned, her long curls sprawled across her back. She looked over her shoulder and gave a sad smile before disappearing and I gripped the letter in an attempt to hold back my tears until later. My head was thick and woolly and I replayed our goodbye as I walked. If I was a man I'd have pulled her from her aunt and we would have run, hand in hand, away from Barley Cove, hitched to the ferry and travelled stowaway to Pembroke. Maybe if I went back, knocked on the door, there would still be time. The rumble of an engine approached and I moved to a grass verge. It was the Hillman, the man and Cora's aunt in the front, and Cora in the back. She looked back as the car drove on and we held each other's gaze, not bothering to wipe away tears. The car disappeared from sight, and then she was gone.

Westwood was the only place I could think to go. Word would be around school by now about what had happened. There would be calling and staring. The last thing I wanted to do was face those eejits. The playground was empty and the tyre swing hung motionless below the stout oak; the spot where I'd sit and swing whilst Cora chatted away, sometimes about America, other times, Shakespeare. When Cora talked, everything was all right. How could I face the silence? My fingers crept to the sealed envelope she'd given me. By its thinness it must have only been a single page.

I used my thumb to open it and scanned the letter hurriedly for words like love. I spotted one, smiled and began reading.

Anthony

They're sending me to England, and I may not see you before I go. There was no way I could leave without letting you know what was going on. Back in the States, me and this girl Molly Regan stole the school master-key from a dumb teacher who left them hanging from a store-room door. Some kid in class told the Head so Molly hid the keys in a toilet cistern. They could never prove who'd taken them, but when the school was burgled the Head informed my parents I'd been seen with the key. Molly and I had been in trouble before so Mom and Dad sent me to Ireland.

Being caught with you and Tom O'Leary's body was the last straw for them, even though we're innocent.

Since meeting you at Jimmy's funeral you've been the best friend anyone could have wished for. More than that, the way we talk and laugh and never say harsh words to one another, well, I think I love you. It's the first time I've ever felt this way.

There's not much time now, but here's the address in England:

18 East Grove

Sherwood Rise

Nottingham

They're not going to keep us apart. It's going to be hard, Anthony, but we'll get through it – somehow.

Cora o x o

"O X O," I said, "Hug, kiss, hug." My eyes flicked to the top of the letter and I read it through once more. My skin felt tight on my cheeks where my tears from earlier had dried. Now it felt although my heart was smiling. I swayed on the tyre swing re-reading her words. That she had never loved a boy, except me, was all I could think of. She was gone now though.

Maybe I could get to the ferry point and stop her leaving. Millie.

I wasn't supposed to be at the farm until tomorrow.

Mr Bray said I could work every other day, now that we'd got on top of things. It was market day so Jimmy's dad was away. Apart from church, I'd never seen Mrs Bray anywhere but inside their house, so I hid among the hay bales until I was sure the coast was clear. The familiar smell of sweet straw reminded me of the times Jimmy and I had talked inside these red walls. Jimmy had a Swiss Army knife that he would use on a piece of wood picked up from the forest. He'd strip the bark as we talked, prepping the wood to carve later. Only once did he show me a finished piece - a snake that he kept hidden in the hayloft so that his parents wouldn't accuse him of being the anti-Christ. The ladder was already positioned against the loft floor and I trod each rung for the first time since Jimmy's death. In the top left hand corner of the loft were the empty cans and containers that were kept just in case. I rummaged through them until my hand settled on the warm wood, the soft curves and smooth python-shaped head, protruding eyes and beginnings of a fork tongue. I held the snake close thinking about how much of Jimmy was in it. His hands had breathed life into a block of wood, like a wizard waving a star-ended wand over a branch, leaving trails of glitter that would clear to reveal a life wriggling before its astonished crowd. Jimmy's spirit coursed along the grain and swirled in the knots like the stream behind the Bray's, the one that pooled further down the hill. The pool where Mr O'Callaghan from the bike shop had seen Jimmy pull out a salmon with his bare hands, perhaps raising it triumphantly in front of a companion other-than-me. The thought of the stranger with Jimmy that day forced me to push the wood away as if the python had turned into an electric eel. It landed on the hay, its magic dissolved. Leaving the carving behind, I scrambled to the loft ladder, which bowed in complaint at my weight.

Outside it had started to rain. In the paddock Millie looked up and munched green grass. Poor Millie, it wasn't her fault. After I opened the gate she walked faithfully to me. Small white puffs came out of her nose as she lowered her head in a slow walk.

"Come on girl, let's get you dry." Her harness was slippery with rain so I took the ring by the side of her mouth. In her stall she steamed a little until I rubbed her down to rid her of the wet.

"You're all I've got now, Millie." Her saddle, hooked on the wall, wore a layer of dust and I took a soft greasy cloth to return its lustre. "Bet that Mr Bray never takes you out."

"Tony!" Mr Bray stood at the barn entrance.

"Sir, the rain, I thought of Millie."

"You're not in trouble. Wanted to talk to you about the horse anyway."

Millie dropped her head into her trough and I approached Mr Bray, shaking out the lint cloth.

"Let's sit down, Tony, over here." Mr Bray took me to a hay bale, reached into his pocket and took out a pouch of tobacco. Slowly he stuffed his pipe. He lit the tobacco with a long match and puffed several times before blowing out the match and dropping it into his pocket. He puffed some more and then removed the stem from his mouth. "See now Jimmy's not here, that horse moons day and night for him. There's no life for her on this farm anymore. You're about the only person she sees, Tony, and I know you've not ridden her since Jimmy went." He puffed on the pipe again, surveying Millie as she watched us. "They're paying good money for Irish cobs at the moment, so I've seen at market."

Then I realised what he was saying. He wanted to

sell Millie. "Sir, I was going to ride her tomorrow, I've cleaned her tack today."

"That's as maybe, lad, but how long will it be before you'll have interests of your own away from the farm, from Millie, from Jimmy's memory?"

I stood. "You can't sell her Mr Bray, I've lost Jimmy and now Cora's gone …"

He cut me off, "Cora, who's Cora? I've no idea what you're talking about. The horse will be sold and that's an end to it."

Mr Bray stood and looked me in the face. "Get yourself home," he said firmly, and left me in the barn with lungs fit to burst and fists clenched with rage.

Millie neighed. "You're coming with me," I said, and started to prepare her for a ride. Usually the straps would make my hands hurt as I pulled them through loops and measured how tight everything should be, comfortable enough for her and safe enough for me. Now I geared her up with speed and dexterity as if all the earlier times had been merely drills.

Once on her back I wobbled for a moment, having forgotten just how high you are when in the saddle. I turned her left and she responded gracefully, letting me lead her from the barn. Mr Bray was gone so I urged Millie on, the clip clop of her hooves on the farm-yard floor. We'd have to get away before the Brays heard Millie. Speeding up I took her forward and she cleared the fence, taking up a gallop through the mud and young crops. It was the first time we'd jumped without Jimmy. He would be the one who reassured me Millie wouldn't throw me, and I wouldn't jump without him there. Now though, as we sped onwards it was as if Millie had always been my horse, as if Jimmy had been the one that taught me how to ride her, but really she was mine – faithful, gentle and kind.

The gate on the other side was open and I slowed Millie to take her safely along the lane. I realised I had been out all day. It was as if I had lost time, like dozing in front of the television at the start of a film and waking up when it was finishing. By now Cora would probably be on the ferry. Even with the means to follow her then it was doubtful they'd let me cross with a horse, and there was no way I could just leave Millie at the dock. I'd never been to Cork harbour but I knew it was a long way and it would probably be morning if travelled to it on horse back. Millie stopped and tore up wild grass from the road side and chewed, thistles and all. I'd have to drive there. Driving couldn't be that difficult; I'd driven the tractor at the Brays before. I could take the car once Dad was asleep.

First I'd have to get Millie settled. We had no stable at home so I thought about taking her to Tom O'Leary's and hiding her in the outhouse. Then I thought better of it and decided to stay away from Tom's. The bracken-filled field near home would be okay, so we trotted on.

The gate had to be jumped as it was seized with rust and strangling weeds.

"You'll be safe here tonight, Millie. I'll come and check on you later." I hauled her saddle away from her back and hid it among the weeds.

It was dark by the time I reached home and my dinner was ready. Mam seemed to believe I'd been at school as usual, and Dad wasn't there. Once Mam was in her bath I went out to check on Millie and took her two sweet buns. "Not sure when I'll be back, Millie, but you'll be okay here."

That night I rested on my bed, waiting for the house to fall into silence. A rapid thumping woke me at ten-thirty, the unmistakable thud of a fist on the back door.

"Where's my horse? That boy of yours!" Mr Bray.

Millie, Mr Bray, the Barber field. Oh no, I couldn't believe I'd stolen his horse. It was bad enough when the ewe escaped. I thought he was going to beat me senseless that day – now I'd aggravated him on purpose. Mam broke my feelings of self pity:

"Tony!"

The kitchen was still warm from dinner as my bare feet padded the tiles. Mr Bray was standing by the kitchen table wearing a donkey jacket and woolly hat. Mam was filling the kettle in her dressing gown but I knew this was no social visit.

"Where's the horse?" said Mr Bray.

"Tony, what's going on?" asked Mam.

Dad appeared. "Is there a fire?"

"Your son has stolen my horse!"

"Whoa now, that's quite an accusation," said Dad.

"Well it's a darn coincidence then that I say to him this afternoon I'm selling the beast and then tonight she's gone."

"Tony, why were you at the farm this afternoon? Haven't you been to school?" asked Mam gently.

Dad stepped forward. "Have you taken Millie?"

"I have."

"What have you done with her?" asked Mr Bray.

"She's in the Barber field."

"What Barber field?"

"The one you damn O'Learys stole from us."

"Tony, I won't have that language in this house." Mam pushed a chair under the table. It screeched along the tiles and emphasised her authority.

"What in God's name are you talking about? The O'Learys stole the field. What field?"

I looked back to Mr Bray. "The one my dad wanted

to buy but you wouldn't let us have."

Dad frowned. "Tony, your mother has warned you and now I'm warning you. If you keep that mouth going I'll have a good hiding ready for you in no time."

"I think the boy means the field between this lane and the next. I'm going to get my horse. I'll leave you two with him." Mr Bray left, and Mam and Dad glared at me.

Dad spoke first. "Tony, horse stealing is a serious offence. Mr Bray could go to the police. What's got into you?"

"He was going to sell Millie!"

"Why shouldn't he? The horse belongs to him!" My father looked serious and it was pointless arguing.

Perhaps Mam would intervene. I turned to her: "Mr Bray wants to send Millie to the knacker's yard."

"Tony, he'll sell her for work. Come here." Mam put her arms around me and I hugged her back, my hands slipping against her silk gown.

Dad left the kitchen when I started to cry. Mam held me close. There was no way I could take Dad's car now. He'd kill me. I thought about Millie being collected by Mr Bray, packed into a horse box and taken away. "I bet it was Mr Bray who killed Jimmy," I said, once the tears had let up some.

seven

Dad's punishment was for me to write a letter of apology to Mr Bray. When I thought about what to say, sorry was easy enough, even if I didn't mean it. What was hard, was putting any feeling into it, so I asked Mam for help and we spent the morning at the kitchen table, talking and writing until Mam was satisfied that I wasn't losing my mind and it was just Cora going that had upset me.

Cora's letter was the only thing that could make me feel better. I read it through again and again, until her warmth came back to me. Did she know I was thinking of her? Perhaps if I closed my eyes I could read her thoughts. It was the only way I could get to sleep. The next day my head would be fuzzy from a night of disturbing dreams. One being of my hands covered in blood, trying to find a sink to wash them in.

Going to school became increasingly difficult in the days that followed Cora's leaving. The nightmares that woke me in the night caused me to oversleep. I had to dash out without breakfast more often than not. My mind would wander during class and I had no appetite for lunch. Before Cora left, I was relieved when the final bell rang; now there was nothing to look forward to. It was like I'd gone back to when Jimmy died, five months ago. I was lonely.

It was difficult to speak to anyone at school, because I think some of them felt sorry for me and didn't know what to say so just ignored me altogether. I saw little point in going to school then. I plucked up enough courage to go to registration, convincing my parents and form tutor that all was as it should be, but then at the first bell I'd leave the school and go to Westwood to be alone and try and clear my head.   I made sure I had an extra layer of clothes under my parka to keep warm during the day. It was a Thursday morning, where a fine rain and a still atmosphere muffled the sound of the any traffic and prompted drivers to switch on their headlights. A squashed rabbit on the road made me wince - my eyes wouldn't let it be. It was a fresh kill, its innards burst through onto the tarmac. Jimmy's laugh echoed in my head.   I looked over my shoulder. There was no-one there.

At Westwood the sky showed an iridescent layer that held slate-blue cloud. Over a puddle the pulley sagged in the middle of the wire, like a pendant on a chain. The tyre-swing hung motionless offering shelter from the rain, and the rope creaked against the oak as I swayed gently to and fro, tracing lines in the dry soil with the toe of my shoe.

Over the last several months I'd seen Cora nearly every day; even if only a few rows ahead of me in class. She was the most beautiful creature I had ever laid eyes on.   I couldn't stay here, Westwood felt haunted, first by Jimmy and then by Cora. With my hood up I left by the gate and turned in the opposite direction to home. The path meandered gently until I reached Hungry Hill. I remembered a rock face up there that Jimmy and I had found a couple of summers ago, beneath it a cave. From there I could watch Barley Cove, without Barley Cove watching me.   The slope was steeper than I'd expected and I found myself mostly climbing. Sheep spotted the hillside like snowy baubles on a Christmas tree, jumping further up the hill the nearer I came. On the coarse wet grass, my shoes slipped backwards, forcing me to cling to wild tufts of heather, prickly against my slimy skin. Nuggets of sheep dung seemed to appear at what seemed like every step, and once on my hands, I gave up trying to avoid it. Somehow I felt stronger physically than I had when Jimmy and I last did this climb. Working on the farm had bulked me up. My arms pulled me with less effort than before, my biceps expanding and contracting fluidly.

A flat ledge gave me a chance to sit and rest and I looked out over Barley Cove. Tom O'Leary's house was hidden beneath a clump of trees. His herd grazed gently, the pebble beach beyond, then the grey sea. She was over it, on land not even visible from Ireland, stretched away from me as if at the other end of a taut elastic-band. If only someone would catapult her back to me. At least it wasn't as far as America, Mam had said.

Mr Bray had talked about Nottingham from time to time. It was rare I listened, but rather followed the tone of his voice and nodded from time to time in the appropriate spots, just like my father would do with Mam as he read the paper. Eventually she'd stop and say, "Are you listening to me?" and that would catch him out, having to answer. Still, some of what Mr Bray said must have stuck because I pictured Nottingham Cathedral with its gleaming pews and mosaic floors, just as Jimmy's dad had described it. That was how his brothers had described it to him he'd said, never having set a foot out of Cork. Now I could see Cora in the Cathedral, in her red coat, her ringlets over the black velvet collar, as pretty as the day I fell in love with her. After Mass, I wondered if they'd all pile back to someone's house for tea and cake, before going home to cook Sunday dinner.

I didn't want to be on Hungry Hill, alone and cold. Cora should be next to me; describing the view, chatting about Jimmy, holding my hand, the way she used to, our fingers weaved into each others'. I wanted to lean into her neck and smell her skin, warm against my cold nose. What if I never saw her again? A sharp stone I'd been picking around came loose and I slung it, full whack, in the direction of the sea.

The wind pushed against my face and I stood to walk on, away from home. Away from my parents, separated but living together, not one iota of union between them - the gap where I lived. Mam talked to me, Dad talked to me, but they never talked to me together. Dad would cut in and change the subject as Mam was talking, as if she wasn't there.

"Beth is seeing her nephews this evening, Tony, would you come with me to …"

"Tony, how are things at the Brays' farm?"

Then Mam would shout at him and say he was interrupting. Dad would insist he couldn't do anything right and then drop his paper and head out to the hotel. Even if I told Dad every day how things were on the farm, he would always cut in and ask whenever Mam had something to say about Beth. Perhaps he thought Mam liked Beth more than him. Either way, it seemed I was little more than a pawn in their game. Away from them meant I could spend time with myself and not have to coddle Mam or defend Dad. If Cora was here with me then I'd be grateful, no matter if we argued or picked petty fights. My parents didn't know how lucky they were to be able to reach out and touch, to kiss, or cuddle, why wouldn't they just do that? Isn't that what people in love were supposed to do?

The grass bedded down as I trod and became squelchy underfoot. Head lowered, I cursed the wind that was driving cold rain into my ears and down the back of my neck. A dog's bark made me look up, and in the distance I saw a figure disappear into a cluster of trees. I followed and found a small dirt track with footprints in the mud. The trail led to an overhang of fir trees stemming from a rock face; their dropped pine needles dry on the ground. Ahead, a stone building sat among thick ferns, its roof carpeted in luscious green moss. An old tin dustbin sat at the building's corner, its corrugated lid tilting, ready to fall at the slightest nudge. There was one window, heavily curtained, blocking out any view of the Atlantic beyond. Only six or so feet to the building's side was a sheer wooded drop to a ledge far below. I turned round and a dog barked.

"Hey!"

I looked over my shoulder and recognised at once the long grey-hair tied back in a pony tail, leather waistcoat and silver-haired face.

The hermit on the hill, Dominic O'Leary.

"What are you doing here? This is private property." His brow was stern.

"Sorry, sir, I was walking on the hill, saw a figure, followed you."

The hermit took several paces forward. "You're Tony Barber aren't you? Jimmy's friend."

"Yes, sir."

His face changed to softness and I breathed a sigh of relief.

"Some day to be walking in the hills. Had enough of it down there have you?" He pointed with his thumb in the direction of Barley Cove.

"Yes, sir. Been thinking about Jimmy, sir."

"Dominic. That's my name."

"Sorry."

"Think about him a lot do you?"

"I do."

"Look at the state of you. Come inside and warm up, I'll make a hot drink."

A fat collie had been watching from behind Dominic. "This is Amy. Leave her be, she's not used to strangers." Dominic's pony tail came to his waist and was bound with a leather shoe lace. The last time he'd cut his hair was probably the last time Amy had herded sheep.

Inside Dominic made for the fireplace, took a poker and turned the embers. He placed small pieces of chopped wood over them and lit the wood with a match until they caught. Then he lifted the lid on a pot over the fire, peered in and closed it again. "There's enough in there for tea." Dominic pulled a stool forward, took my coat and hung it over a worn chair to dry. "Get yerself warm, lad."

I pushed my hands towards the heat and felt instantly at home. The gas fire at our house gave out fake heat compared to this.

Dominic cuffed the curtain. "It won't rain again before dark or dinner," he said. He dragged his loose heels along the stone floor, his unlaced boots flopping around his ankles. Beside the fire he reached for the boiled pot and poured hot water into a battered teapot.

"Take off your shoes if you want," said Dominic.

My arms were coming alive again but my feet were so wet that they were painfully cold. I took off my socks too and crept my feet greedily towards the heat. Dominic handed me a blue and white chipped mug. The tea was sweet and felt good on my empty stomach. The warmth of the room mixed with the smell of turf gave me a light, heady feeling. This is what it must have been like for Dominic all the time, alone here in this shack, sheltered from the cruel weather by the craggy rocks and thick, heavy-set trees. The fire crackled and birds started singing, a sure sign the rain had stopped. I became conscious that my face must be smeared with mud and used the sleeve of my sweater to wipe any muck away.

Dominic looked over at the window again, perhaps to give me privacy. "See that now, the sun is coming out." His kind expression was illuminated by the fire.

I wished I'd been here with Jimmy before he died.

"So what's the problem?"

"I didn't know you were Jimmy's uncle until his funeral. He never talked about you."

"Out of sight, out of mind," said Dominic, and he stoked the fire.

"I'm starting to forget now, what it was like when he was alive," I said.

"You two were close weren't you?"

"We did everything together. The first memory I have of him is my first day at school. Mam says we were friends at nursery but it's that day at school that I remember most, when the teacher asked us to write our name and everyone else seemed to know how to do it apart from me. I couldn't write the letter A at the beginning of Anthony. Jimmy said he couldn't spell James and that Jimmy was much easier to remember. He asked me what was short for Anthony and I said Tony, so he asked the teacher to show me how to spell Tony and by the end of the day I was writing my name. It stuck, and everyone starting calling me that." I looked into the fire. "Except Cora."

Dominic gave a small laugh. "So there's a girl."

"Was a girl."

"Yes, it makes sense now; you and this Cora girl found my brother dead. That's what they're saying in the village anyhow."

"I'm sorry about your brother."

"The priest found you there?"

"He did."

Dominic shook his head. "Priest knew brother Tom very well."

"The priest said Tom O'Leary wouldn't have been found until the next day if Cora and I hadn't got there first. He was there himself though."

"Like I say, the priest knew my brother very well." Dominic lifted the teapot and filled our mugs. "Jimmy always called me Uncle Dom," he said.

"So you used to see him then?"

"Until I moved up here. Would've been around the time you two started school. First time I saw him was when he was one-day old. His mother, my sister, passed him to me all wrapped up in a white cotton blanket. It was like a waterfall of love washed over me." Dominic stared into the fire.

A beetle scurried past my stool and into the darkness. When I talked to Mam about Jimmy she nodded her head, but it was as if I was talking about a pop star whose music she didn't really know. Even Cora, who knew and liked Jimmy, didn't share the bond I had with him, the same bond Dominic had.

Dominic spoke. "Why were you and Cora at Tom's?"

The story we'd given Father Molony and our relatives didn't seem appropriate to tell Dominic. I sensed he could spot a lie from a hundred yards. In a way I liked that because it meant I could trust him not to be dishonest with me. Dominic struck me as the kind of person that people told their secrets to. It was worth a try, besides, he might understand and not being able to talk about what had happened was driving me mad. "It was when Tom fell into the table drunk at Jimmy's funeral and said Jimmy was better off out of this sham. It got me thinking and the only way to find out more was to get Tom drunk. I took a bottle of left-over

whiskey from the Brays and gave it to Tom. The plan
was to wait until he passed out and then search his house
for clues. But then ..." A lump was rising in my throat
and my eyes filled with tears.

"Never mind, son," said Dominic, "I know the rest."

"Finding him like that was horrible," I wiped my
eyes. "If I hadn't given him the whiskey."

"He'd be dead anyway," said Dominic.

"What do you mean?"

"It's not your fault my brother's dead, Tony. There
are forces at work here beyond our control. Tom got
what was coming to him."

"Did Tom murder Jimmy?"

"No he didn't." Dominic turned his attention to his
sheepdog and smoothed the crown of her head in slow
strokes. The dog looked over to me with her one blue
eye, one brown, the tip of her tail brushed the floor in a
lazy wag.

"Have you been to confession about the whiskey
stealing?"

"I haven't."

"Why don't you make an appointment to see the
priest, speak to him man to man. This one might take
too long for the confessional. Don't want to leave the
likes of Peggie Sheehan waiting on bended knee now
do we?" Dominic winked and rubbed underneath
Amy's chin.

Confession had to be the worst part of being a Catholic.
The box always smelled of fusty hymn books and I
could never remember what it was I should be
confessing. Being cheeky to my mam or taking the
Lord's name in vain; it was the same every time. After
giving me a penance of one *Our Father* and five *Hail
Mary's* the priest would bless me and then sweep the

curtain closed across on his side of the grill. Just when you thought he'd not recognised your voice he'd say, "Bye Tony", or "Say hello to your parents, Tony." It shouldn't have made me nervous speaking to him face to face, but I was worried in case he saw something in my eyes that told him I wasn't sorry for what I'd done.

The housekeeper opened the presbytery passage and left me waiting in the hallway. It was dark inside with the only sound a ticking clock. A crucifix with a bowl of holy water beneath it hung on the wall. I dipped my fingers into the water and crossed myself just as Father Molony appeared and joined me in the hall.

"Hello Tony. Are you well?"

"I am thank you, Father."

"Through here," he said, and led me to a room at the front of the house.

The room was barely furnished with just a table and two chairs at the window. Father Molony gestured for me to sit and we faced each other.

"Bless me Father for I have sinned."

"How long is it since your last confession?"

"Four months, Father."

"And what is it that you'd like to confess?"

"Well Father, I did a terrible thing and I think a man died because of it."

"Do you mean Tom O'Leary?"

"I do. I took a bottle of whiskey from the Brays and gave it to Tom. It was supposed to make him go to sleep, but…"

"But it killed him you think?"

I looked at the table top to avoid the priest's eyes.

"Do you think Satan made you do it?" asked the priest.

I looked at him. "It was my own will, Father."

"Now why would you want to go do a thing like

that?" The priest leaned forward, his breath smelled of peppermint.

"I think Tom O'Leary was involved in Jimmy Bray's death."

The priest inhaled quickly then started coughing, he put his right hand to his mouth, which was bruised in yellow, his knuckles scabbed. Catching my gaze he dropped his hand down and brought the left to his mouth. He coughed furiously for a minute or so and seemed unable to catch his breath.

The housekeeper tapped on the door. "Do you need me, Father?"

Father Molony waved his hand toward him and I called for the housekeeper to come in.

"I'll get you some water, Father," she said. On return she fussed around Father Molony, helping him hold the glass as he sipped as if he were a small child. He let out small dry coughs as she rubbed his back and his face was red and glistened with beads of sweat. He tugged at his collar and wiped his forehead with the back of his hand. Assured that the priest was okay now, the housekeeper left, leaving the glass of water on the table. Father Molony reached for it again, forgetting his injured hand. The colour of the bruising meant it could have been a few days old.

"Now where were we?" he said, straightening himself in his chair.

"I forget, Father," I said.

"The whiskey and Tom O'Leary."

"Father, can I have my penance and go into the church and pray please?"

"Tony, if you think it's your fault Tom O'Leary is dead then you need to ask God for forgiveness, to be sorry for what you've done. You should try and think of ways to repair the hurt you have caused, to his family and to God."

I looked to the tabletop again. It wasn't sorrow I was feeling. It was rage.

eight

That's the thing about evil, it lurks in the most unlikely places; places where those closest to God are most at risk. The devil took Jimmy and used Tom O'Leary to get him. That was probably why Tom drank, tired of doing the devil's dirty work. The priest though, who did he serve?

The nuns had promised me and Jimmy that as long as we were good Catholics, God would look after us. Jimmy hadn't done anything wrong, but God failed to look after *him*. Father Molony was the one who taught us about doubting Thomas, the reason he's not in the Bible, that he lacked faith, bringing negativity, humiliation and ultimately the end of his own life.

When I closed my eyes, the dark contorted faces were back, stabbing at my forehead. Reaching to the bedside table, I knocked over an open bottle of aspirin. They gushed towards me, like minty *tic tacs*. I swallowed one with water and took a second for good measure. Scooping the pills back into the bottle I thought of Jimmy, alone in space, floating aimlessly like an astronaut separated from his ship. *One day Jimmy, I'll find out what really happened to you.* I waited for the dark images to leave, and fell peacefully asleep.

Morning came and with it a dry mouth. Remnants of my dream, ghostly figures and a river bed, a secret chamber among brown reeds and silt.

I drank a cup of tea at the kitchen window and watched steam rise from the grass as the sun dried the morning dew. A thrush hopped on the lawn and with its beak pulled out a floppy worm.

The night Cora and I found Tom O'Leary dead the

priest had said he checked on Tom every evening because Tom had got steadily worse with the drink since his brother, Dominic, moved up to Hungry Hill. He also said they wouldn't serve Tom in the The Bull anymore, not after what happened. He didn't say *what* had happened.

Brendan Sullivan, the pub landlord, was sweeping the pavement outside The Bull. It was a relief he was there because even though under-eighteens were often seen going into the pub with their parents, they were mostly tourists, and Mr Sullivan was strict about children being in his pub. The only time I'd ever been in The Bull was to bring my dad home one Friday tea-time, before he'd started working at the hotel. We couldn't afford a phone then as my father was tilling the fields with his brother in Adrigole, barely making a living with what Chris Dee paid them. I'd walked into the bathroom at home, without knocking first, and found my pregnant mother standing in the bath, half-clothed with blood running down her leg. Dad left word in the pub and the doctor was at our house by the time we returned. On the day they told me that I wouldn't be having a baby brother or sister anymore, the three of us spent all day on the sofa, my father in the middle with one arm round my mother and the other around me. Every time my mother cried she'd bury her head in my father's neck and he'd stroke her hair. He swore he'd never pray to God again after that.

Brendan Sullivan was propped over his broom. The path barely needed sweeping, but in Barley Cove there were things that just had to be done everyday. "Tony, how are you, young man?"

"I'm fine, thank you, Mr Sullivan."

"And your mother, how's she these days?"

"Well enough, thank you, sir. She's been worried

lately because of Jimmy Bray dying, then Tom O'Leary after that."

"Was sudden, granted, both of them going the way they did. Jimmy Bray, God rest his soul." Mr Sullivan crossed himself. "His uncle though. They say don't speak ill of the dead but in this case I'll make an exception. The bane of my life he was, a real pain in the wotsit." He shook his head and began sweeping again.

"Father Molony said he was trouble sure enough."

"Barred in the end he was." The landlord stopped sweeping again. "Spouting stuff I wouldn't repeat."

"Father Molony said he took it a step too far. What did he say?"

"Well, now… to be sure, it's not my place to say. He wasn't clear… just madness from the drink, Tony."

"He liked a drop according to Father Molony," I said.

"He did indeed. Killed him in the end though, but God knows everyone round here tried to get him off it. There's those that can't stop you see, and he was one of 'em." Mr Sullivan left the broom against the wall and wiped his hands on the back of his trousers. Large spots of rain dropped and gave the swept walkway a polka-dot look. The landlord went into to the pub lobby and hooked the door to the wall so that it stayed open. "Say hello to your parents for me, Tony."

"I will."

A rainbow arched from The Bull to the other side of Hungry Hill convincing me this was only a shower and a hood would do. Half way up the Hill the weather changed, bringing drizzle and a blustery wind that made the sheeps' dripping wool swing like ropes beneath them. Soon it would be time for shearing and no doubt I'd be called to help Mr Bray on the farm.

Dominic was inside with the door to his home open. Out of courtesy I knocked, but Amy had already barked and Dominic knew I was there.

"Wondered when I'd see you again, Tony Barber. Come in, come in, tell me all about it." He was sitting in the same chair as before, whittling down a small piece of light coloured wood. "Can you carve?" he asked.

"Jimmy could," I said.

"The tourists in Bantry pay good money for carvings; keeps food in my belly." The shavings curled around his feet and made the fire spit when they flew into it. Amy went to Dominic and sat beside him.

"The priest, Father Molony, one of his hands is bashed up."

"What do you make of it?" Dominic asked, all the while his focus on the wood.

"When I said to the priest I thought Tom might have something to do with Jimmy's death he had a massive coughing fit – I thought he was having an asthma attack."

"My brother didn't kill Jimmy, I told you that."

"And I believe you, but what was Tom hiding?"

Dominic nicked small pieces from the wood. From my angle it looked like the ears of a rabbit.

"I went to see Brendan Sullivan at The Bull," I said.

"What did he have to say about it?"

"That he barred Tom from the pub for spouting rubbish."

Dominic blinked, put the wood and knife on the floor then rubbed his hands together looking into the fire. He ran his hand over his grey pony tail and I took this to mean he was holding something back. I asked about the photos at Tom's, how they were of Mrs Bray and Jimmy, but nobody else. Dominic shifted in his seat. For a moment I thought I must have overstayed my welcome and instinctively reached for my coat. He stood and indicated with his hand that I should remain seated. Then he went to the table, its top scrubbed white as bone. He flattened his knuckles to the table and shifted his weight onto his arms like a slim, silver-backed gorilla.

"Likes his own kind too much that one," he said.

I was puzzled for a moment. It still didn't explain why there weren't photos of other family members in Tom's house.

"He couldn't leave his sister alone you see. Always at her he was, ever since she was small. Then she started growing up and they'd play together in secret. I was never part of it – like there was something wrong with me and they didn't like me."

I started to see why Dominic chose to live alone for a second, but what he said next made me choke on my drink.

"She got pregnant."

I stopped breathing so the tea wouldn't end up in my airway. "Tom was…"

Dominic nodded.

I started to cough. I moved my mug onto the floor and covered my mouth as I spluttered all the air and tea away. My eyes started watering. I wanted to speak before the thoughts grew in my mind, and all I could do was croak. I breathed shallow breaths, wanting to cough so hard.

Dominic slammed the tabletop with his fist. He lowered his head and I could see his shoulders move up and down slowly as he took deep breaths. He walked back to the seat beside the fire.

There was no way I could leave now, walk back down the mountain and go home pretending nothing had happened. "Who else knows?"

"Our parents of course, but they're dead now. Me, my sister, Tom and…" he stopped."

"There's someone else. Who?"

Dominic remained quiet.

"Did Jimmy know?"

"Jimmy came up here only the once," he continued. "Last September it would have been. I welcomed him. It was a joy it really was. But I saw he was tangled in knots. I asked him to sit, right there where you are. He kept pacing though, up and down, wringing his hands, saying he wanted to kill his Uncle Tom, that I should help him. He started talking all-strange, about putting an end to it all. It struck me. I knew what the boy was trying to say. He must have seen the recognition on my face, because he broke down, fell to his knees on that there stone floor and sobbed. The day before I'd gone to buy bread from O'Shea's and passing Tom's I saw Jimmy come out of his house. I called over to Jimmy, he turned and looked at me blankly before he ran away, back in the direction of the farm. I thought he was plain scared of me. I went over to Tom's to see what the boy was there for. Tom was in and it was obvious he'd been drinking. He said he'd told Jimmy the truth and I became angry. Tom started on about our sister. He slurred into my face and called her a whore. So I knew, when Jimmy cried here, Tom had relieved his own guilt at the expense of his own nephew. His own son."

"My sister always referred to Tom you see, as Jimmy's special uncle, and it worked well enough for a while. Tom was supposed to stay away from Jimmy but he blackmailed my sister and said he'd tell Jimmy he was his father if she didn't agree to let Jimmy visit him. All started last spring. Dominic went to the window, held back the curtain and looked out over the cove. "And ended last winter".

Amy walked to the window and sniffed at Dominic's hand. He smoothed her head and she sat.

Another piece of the patchwork made itself known. Not long after me and Jimmy went back to school last September, Jimmy became ill and started missing class. The teacher wouldn't tell me what was wrong so I went to the farm to find out. Mrs Bray said Jimmy was in bed. He then came to the door and his eyes were red, their lids puffy. There were shadows chiselled into his cheeks and he was stooped, as if carrying a log on his shoulders. Mrs Bray sent him back to his room and said it was a nasty cold he had and I should wait for him to return to school before bothering him again. As I walked to the farm gate I looked up at Jimmy's bedroom window. He was looking down at me. I waved madly but he didn't wave back. The sad expression on his face froze into my memory like a photograph.

When Jimmy did come back to school he spoke very little. Thinking about it now, he was like a dog that had been beaten, slunk low and submissive, his spirit drained away. "I stepped back thinking he wasn't interested in me anymore. It was the time he needed me the most," I said.

"There was nothing anyone could do Tony."

"What about Mr Bray? How does he fit into all this?"

"He knew Tom had told Jimmy, but the Brays are full of pride, so he insisted Jimmy not tell a soul."

"How did Mr Bray become Jimmy's dad I mean?"

Dominic came back beside the fire and scraped wood shavings toward the hearth with his boot. "There's plenty know my sister was in the family way before she married. They all thought Bray was the father. My parents pushed her into marrying him. His family didn't complain – we own most of the land around here; I suppose he was forced into it too. No one asked who the real father was. Thought that would be the end of it when she married him. Tom hit the drink to drown out what he'd done and once Beth Harrington's father knew that one of ours was having relations before she was married, my engagement to Beth Harrington ended. I couldn't stand it; Beth wouldn't come near me after that and my heart was broken, so it was. I came up here. That way I wouldn't have to see her every day." Dominic looked at the floor.

The petals in my mind slowly began to unfurl, and I thought about Beth and how she'd reacted when she'd seen Dominic at Jimmy's funeral.

Dominic spoke, "Jimmy was the only good thing that came out of it all. I loved that boy with my heart and soul, and the day I became his Godfather I started praying for him, and have done so on my rosary every night since. That poor boy." Dominic wiped his eyes and lowered his face into his chest.

"I loved him too," I heard myself say. It was the first time I'd been with anyone else that really seemed to care about Jimmy as much as I did.

Dominic looked at me intensely and I eased back on my stool a little to try and break his stare.

I bent to pick up my cup, tea had slopped down its sides after my choking fit. I took a swig to break the silence, not really wanting any more. "Those few months before he died, I knew deep down something was wrong."

Dominic glanced at me sideways.

"I hate Tom O'Leary! He killed Jimmy!"

"Jimmy killed himself, Tony!"

"What? What do you mean?"

"Took his mother's *Valium* and ended it all, God rest his soul."

"No, Jimmy wouldn't do that."

"But he has, Tony, don't you see, it was the only way out for him."

"I can't believe it, I just can't believe it." Air wouldn't go to my lungs and I heaved for breath whilst my eyes misted. For a moment I was stunned, a dizzy feeling had me rest my forehead in my hands, my ears closed to the sounds around me, unable to hear anymore, my limbs heavy with refusal to move. If a fire had broken out in the shack at that moment I'd have been burned to death on the stool, my body unable to carry me from danger. The fluid silence of shock gripped me with octopus-like tentacles.

It made no sense. "Did he take the tablets then go for a swim? He was a fine swimmer, he wouldn't drown!"

"Tony, I've said enough, I can offer you more tea but I'm sorry lad, I've caused you too much pain."

"I have to go, get home." I grappled for my coat, everything focused on getting out of what now seemed like a place from hell. Mammy. I needed my mam, her touch, her smile, the safety of her hug.
"I need to go home."

Dominic shook his head but let me go without too much fuss. There couldn't be many people Dominic spoke to up here. Maybe that was why he told me what he knew. Being able to talk about Jimmy, not being able to stop because the words refused to be locked away anymore; like when I told Cora I'd found Jimmy dead – because I had to tell someone and she was all I had.

The smell of cloyed earth hung in the air and a magpie

hopped into the road before taking flight. I wanted to see Dominic again, to help me unravel the spaghetti in my head. I'd woken this morning at four-thirty, with a pain in my stomach that had made my legs shake. I'd felt cold but all the windows were shut, and Mam had pulled a patched blanket over me in the night. Dark, contorted faces had floated behind my eyes and then Tom O'Leary's red face, his pudgy fingers reaching for the bottle and the pool of blood coming from his head. That's when I'd started shaking all over. In the bathroom I'd been unable to throw up so I'd gone back to bed and slept fitfully for what seemed like only minutes at a time, until I realised the only way to stop the nightmares was stay awake.

On the track that led to Dominic's there was a cluster of berries waiting to be picked but the nausea lingered, quashing my appetite. A small stream of smoke drifted from the hut's chimney, convincing me Dominic must be home. I hesitated before knocking. There were voices from inside; one male, one female. It sounded like whoever was in there was getting ready to leave so I moved back snapping a twig beneath my foot. Amy barked so I scrambled round the back of the hut and hid behind the blue tub that caught rainwater from the guttering. The latch clicked and I squatted down further when I heard footsteps rustle leaves. Bobbing my head round the tub I saw a woman in a navy coat, hands in pockets and her red hair tied neatly in a bun. It was Beth Harrington.

If I knocked now he'd know I'd seen Beth leaving. It would mean he might have to lie about why she was there and I didn't want to give him reason for doing so. To prevent Amy barking I followed Beth from a distance. She turned right at the end of the dirt track and led me down a new route with a softer gradient and well-worn path. It brought me to a little jitty that ran between Joe Harrington's butcher shop and Monk's Garage. Beth could be up and down that hill all day and no-one but her would know. Once I was sure she'd gone into her father's shop I turned round and headed back up the track. Without Beth as a distraction I had to stop several times and hunch over with my hands on my thighs to support me, thinking I wanted to be sick, but nothing happened.

A trickle of smoke was still rising from Dominic's chimney but after knocking once with no reply I knew Dominic wasn't home; so I wandered the hill looking for him, thinking of Cora and wishing she was with me. My heart was beating powerfully until it hurt, my eardrums expanding and contracting with the whoosh of blood that sped through me. It was the same just after Jimmy had died; the feelings that disrupted my life to the point where the doctor diagnosed me as suffering from anxiety, but there was nothing he could do. Had it been less severe then, or had I just forgotten how disturbing it really was? When Cora came into my life the feelings of hopelessness disappeared, but now it was back, gripping me in its tendrils, ready to start eating me alive from the inside, until I died a slow, agonising death.

Led Zeppelin resounded through my head — the music Jimmy had got me listening to:

If it keeps on raining, levee's gonna break

The discomfort grabbed my gut again and I leaned against a tree to try and clear my mind until it passed.

Mean old levee taught me to weep and moan

It was Jimmy's favourite track from their fourth album. We'd play it loud in my room with the drums and harmonica crashing like a wailing storm, whooping us into excitement, edging up the volume little by little until the next door neighbour banged on their side of the wall. Then we'd laugh and Jimmy would tell me the story of how the song was first written in 1929 and that Robert Plant had re-written it to make it the band's own. I'd ask him how he knew and he'd tell me his cousin in England read music magazines and would write to Jimmy and tell him about his favourite bands.

An image of Jimmy's back again, his black curls tinted red in the sun, as he walked towards the Bray's barn. Tom mopping his brow before he followed Jimmy and let the barn door close behind them. My heart started racing and I turned and pelted back to Dominic's. The dog barked before I had chance to knock and Dominic appeared, looking at me as I gasped for breath.

"I want to know more," I began. "How Jimmy ended up in the river, who put him there."

"You'd better come in, Tony."

The fire in the hearth was big and orange, reflecting on Dominic's face as he gestured for me to sit. He stoked the flames then ran a hand over the sheepdog's head.

"The papers said Jimmy had water in his lungs. Tom killed him! Held him under water, murdered him!"

"My brother wasn't a murderer, Tony. For sure Jimmy committed a mortal sin. Now leave it be."

nine

The rain spots washed the peaty drowsiness from my
face before I ducked into a bus shelter to wait until the
storm passed. A bus timetable showed two-a-day to
Cork City. It was still early. I could catch the ferry
today. Visitors to the hotel in the cove did it all the
time.

Cora's address was running through my head and
Barley Cove appeared to have shown me all there was
for now. If I caught the bus to Cork and took the boat
train to the ferry, would it hurt anyone? Not Dad for
taking his car, or Mr Bray for his horse. By running I
would arrive home in time to collect the money hidden
under my bed. Nausea passed and adrenaline raced
through my veins.

The rain was bouncing from the ground and the
roads changed to small streams. A car with slapping
windscreen wipers hooted when I made a dash for the
other side. At home the kitchen windows were opaque
with steam so I went inside without knowing if anyone
was in. The house was quiet and I pulled off my clothes
on the way upstairs. My trousers clung to my legs and I
peeled them away before stuffing them in a plastic bag
on the wardrobe floor. From under the bed I took the
old baked-bean tin and counted the money Mr Bray
paid me, not a penny of it spent.   Into my rucksack I
packed the clean socks and underwear Mam left on the
bed. I tugged two clean shirts from hangers, leaving
them to swing to and fro.

The rain eased some and I saw the bus ahead
indicating to leave. My legs pushed hard and I made it
before the driver pulled away.

"That was close," he said, when I bought my fare.

At the back of the bus I raised my knees against the seat in front and propped my bag to hide from any passengers who may join at the next stop. The evidence from Tom's was zipped into the pocket of my rucksack. With it half undone, my fingers plucked out the plastic tubing; it was smooth over my finger tips and stopped me thinking for a while. Watching the blur of green outside, I dropped my knees and rested my head on my bag. My eyelids slid shut.

"Cork!" shouted the driver, waking me up.

I grabbed my bag and went to the front of the bus. "Can you tell me how to get to the boat train please?"

"What do you want with the boat train?"

"I'm meeting a relative, my father couldn't get time off work."

The bus driver reached up and wound the back of his destination sign. "Half a mile that way," he said and pointed. "Follow signs for boat train to the port."

"Thanks. Do you know how long the train journey is?"

"Thought you were meeting someone."

"I'm meeting them at the ferry."

The driver looked at my bag, then reached into his jacket pocket. "Do you have money for the fare?"

"I do, thank you."

"Well, look after yourself now."

The train dropped me at the ferry point. I paid for my ticket and was directed to the foot passenger queue. Cars packed to the gills with suitcases and jackets sat in a line, nose to tail, their families milling around, some smoking, others holding small children. Ahead was the yawning mouth of the B&I *Innisfallen,* its cargo deck filling with artic trucks. There was the stench of warm oil and the sound of gulls. A man with ruddy cheeks and a high vis' jacket was checking foot-passenger tickets. I stood close to a family of Travellers, wondering if I'd pass for their son in the hope it wasn't obvious I was travelling alone.

In the passenger lounge, the family claimed territory by leaving jackets and bags on seats. I chose a seat alongside and left my parka over it to dry before going in search of food. No more than the bar was open - I bought a packet of crisps and a glass of cola for fifty pence.

The boat shuddered over the engines and a small knot tightened in my chest when the ferry began moving out to the grey sea. On the deck, salt water mixed with rain sprayed me and the wind pulled my hair fiercely. Cora's hair must have whipped across her face she stood here, perhaps sticking to the tears on her cheeks. I stayed on deck until the sight of land had gone and all was left to do was sleep.

The ferry arrived in Pembroke Dock that evening and there was no coach to Nottingham available until seven the next morning. I joined the other foot passengers in an all-night café, drinking tea and filling in the crossword puzzle from the day's paper. The Travellers were grouped in one corner, the mother's black hair tousled over her shoulders onto a green velvet blouse. She changed her baby's nappy on a chair next to her. Looking away I watched her two dark-haired toddlers, clambering over their father while he dealt cards to a younger man I took to be his brother. The woman picked up the clean baby and rocked it, her light eyes following the cards intently.

I woke with my head on the table, the warm newspaper beneath my cheek. There was the clatter of cutlery and plates, chairs scraping across the floor. A barrelled-shaped man with a grey moustache and stubbly chin dropped a clean ash tray in front of me, his fingers tips yellowed by tobacco.

The Travellers were rustling bags and pulling on coats and hats. My hand crept to my coat pocket looking for the roll of notes from the baked-bean tin. The money was still there and I was ashamed I'd not trusted my surrogate family. Leaving the sprawled newspaper on the table, I followed the group to the ticket office, where the toddlers pulled at their mother's long skirt, forcing her to drop a heavy travel-bag while holding the infant close to her. Rubbing the baby's back she told the children to sit, but they ignored her and cried to be picked up until the woman sat on the bag herself and let the small ones rest their heads on her lap, all the while rubbing the baby's back and planting little kisses on its bald head.

Behind the kiosk a roller blind sprung open to reveal a middle-aged woman in bifocals.

The older of the two men plunged a hand into his trouser pocket and brought out a hand full of crumpled notes, dotted higgledy-piggledy with loose change. "Good morning, Miss. Can I have tickets for three adults and two children please, one way to Birmingham it is."

The assistant punched his tickets from a machine. She smiled at me whilst the man counted his money. "Thank you there," he said, after she pushed the tickets to him.

"Where are you heading young man?" Her accent was Welsh and I listened closely to catch what she was saying.

"Nottingham please," I answered. "One way, please."

"Do you have the fare from Pembroke to Nottingham?"

"I do," and I took out the role of notes from my pocket.

The woman behind the kiosk leaned forward. "If I were you I'd put your wad away before you're robbed." She nodded towards the Travellers, the older man carrying the heavy bag, and his brother the two children.

"They're my friends," I said in defence, unfolding Irish pound notes from the roll.

"Friends you say. Huh!" Her face crumpled and she straightened out the notes. "Didn't they tell you to change your money? It's pounds sterling over here," she said.

"No. No they didn't tell me." My thoughts ran slowly still drunk from sleep. It would be hours until anywhere opened to change my money. "Getting to Nottingham is really important, ma'am."

The cashier bashed some numbers into a calculator. "I'll take enough to cover your fare and take it to the Bureau de Change before I cash up at lunch time."

"Thank you, thank you very much."

"The coach stops at Birmingham first. You look tired," she said, pushing a ticket my way. "Just don't fall asleep on the bus."

Once on the coach the smell of fried food and stale cigarette smoke made me frown. The journey would take hours and I planned to sleep through it. Barley Cove grew further away by the minute, its golden sandy beach and lush farmland; tied together by the folks I'd known my whole life.

Sleep was difficult with my head against the window and I used the road markings to hypnotise me, the broken white-line converging into one long thread, pulling me closer to Cora, mile by mile.

It was mid afternoon when the coach pulled into

Victoria bus station in Nottingham and my insides must have resembled an empty cave. With no need to wait for a bag from the hold I left the other passengers and the fussing coach driver. A ragged tramp interrupted my reading of bus timetables, asking me for spare change to buy a cup of tea. He smelled of rancid diarrhoea, and I ignored him by moving towards the toilets. They stank of urine, covered up with disinfectant, but there was no-one about, which gave me a chance to brush my teeth.

The tramp wandered in. He preened himself in the mirror, looked at me and laughed. "Pretty is she?" He grabbed his belt and laughed like an evil Santa Claus in rags. His stench wafted over again and I snatched my bag from the sink top and headed out of the toilets, his mocking laughter echoing from the ceramic-tiled walls. Pigeons fluttered from my path as I ran from the station to the main road. Mannequins poised in city fashion gleamed from shop windows, and the sound of music escaped from a pub named The Yorker. A stray dog overtook me, his fur wiry and honey coloured. He cocked his leg against a lamp post and disappeared round the corner. Following him would give me *some* direction at least, and sure enough, below the Victoria Hotel, was a taxi rank. Trouble was, I still had no British money. *Please God don't let Cora live tens of miles from here.*

The ride from the city centre took about ten minutes and I asked the driver to drop me at the bottom of East Grove, in case anyone from Cora's saw me arrive. The cabbie insisted I leave my name and address for having Irish money. He made me promise to go into the firm's office and pay for my ride once I'd some British sterling.

"Name's Dave," he said. "Car 8." He caught my glance in the rear-view mirror and shook his head.

Reaching up, he took a card from behind the sun visor and scribbled on it with a pen. "Here, the address is on the front, my name and car number on the back. Got it?"

"I have, sir," I replied.

"Good. I'll get your bag from the boot."

East Grove was a row of terraced houses sloping up towards larger houses, with a side entrance leading to number eighteen. Holding my knuckles near the glass I took a deep breath. Then I saw her, standing side-ways on, her hair cascading down her back, her delicate fingers holding a book. Tapping lightly on the patterned glass I called her name in my loudest whisper. Her head turned, eyes wide, and her face broke into a smile. It was all I could look at until she stood in front of me, two steps above, wearing a blue dress.

ten

Here, in the milder climate, sparrows perched on the crumbling wall, twitching and hopping against a tie-dyed sky. Sun rays leapt the length of garden, leaving shade beneath the dead-end trees. Next to the dustbin stood a pair of small red wellies, mud spattered, and legless.

On the entry wall Cora kicked the back of her shoes against the brick and listened to me tell her more about stealing Millie and meeting Dominic O'Leary. It hurt to break the news of the circumstances of Jimmy's death to Cora. I wished I could have spared her its horror, but Cora could tell I was holding something back. Her gentle coaxing worked its magic though and telling her brought us closer. We agreed to find out exactly what role the priest played in it all, if merely to discover who dumped Jimmy's body into the river.

We giggled whilst Cora's delicate fingers fit a key into a rusty padlock. It clicked undone and Cora opened the out-house where a white seat-less toilet jutted from the back wall. Cora reached inside and on came a light showing a sack of potatoes and two crates of fizzy pop. There where shelves above the toilet stacked with tins of soup, chopped tomatoes, baked beans and sweet corn. On the ground was a pile of old newspaper with a roll of pink toilet tissue on top.

"This is your new room," said Cora, her face deadpan. The smile cracked through and I knew she was joking. "The kids eat a mile a minute and this is where my cousin stores extra stuff." Cora looked down at a list and began passing me tins and packets. "Bring these in," she said.

"Yes dear."

Cora smiled again, and snapped padlock shut.

With Cora's cousin Phil and his wife Christine we shared the bare bones of what happened, telling them the truth. They were sympathetic and offered me a place to stay. Christine made me phone Ireland though. My mother was emotional, frightened out of her wits she said, but it was agreed by the end of my first day in England I should stay put until arrangements could be made for me to travel back. Deep down I suspected Mam knew it would be safer this way, if they'd insisted I return immediately, the chances were Cora and I could run away.

In the kitchen Christine put cans in cupboards and Cora reached up for a saucepan. "So I'm only allowed to wear dresses and skirts now," Cora chattered. "So I'll act more like a lady."

In the front room the children played in their pyjamas whilst their dad read the racing pages of the paper, his thick black eyebrows dark over heavy lids. The gold Irish Claddagh on his wedding finger glinted from the sunshine pouring in through the window and the ash from his cigarette dripped into an ashtray on the arm of his chair.

A girl and a boy, the children gave me building blocks to add to their tower. We built the tower high until one of them nudged it accidentally-on-purpose, giggling when it toppled.

Cora called us into the back room for Christine's bumper breakfast of bacon, eggs, sausage, beans and mounds of fried bread. The toddlers were sat in high chairs next to their mum with Cora next to me and Phil opposite. Among the clatter of children, busy knives and forks, and Phil pouring tea, Christine's back room held us together in an invisible mesh, where conversations glided and titters of laughter fell in all the right places. At home things didn't fit together but were stilted, happening separately, like a guitar-playing busker missing the rest of his band.

Walking to Saint Mary's, the twins held hands between Cora and me. Outside the church, Phil joined the men and smoked whilst Christine gossiped with the women, their accents from Galway, Belfast and Cork itself. Cora led me into church and we sat together near the back. Families filtered in and the pews filled, Cora whispering the names of people she knew. Two girls smiled when they passed, looked at me and giggled before kneeling and crossing themselves. The bells tinkled and the congregation stood. Father Quaine welcomed us and I thought about Father Molony, his bruised hand and two of his flock dead. Father Molony must have known Tom O'Leary was Jimmy's father. Cora took my hand, I smiled into her soft face and Father Quaine read the Gospel according to Saint Luke.

Merging toward the side with the rest of the congregation, I waited to dip my finger into holy water before exiting Mass. Cora watched as I crossed myself, but ignored the water when it was her turn. She appeared so fearless and free from worry, keen only to head home. Phil came with us leaving Christine and the children with their friends. Cora was giddy and several times Phil asked her to calm down.

"You're not going to believe what you see next, Anthony," she said, at the corner of East Grove.

Clouds gave flicker to the rays of a glimpsing sun, highlighting the wheel spokes of a sports car with a GB sticker. It looked the same as the one I'd seen in the car park at Jimmy's funeral. On the back seat was Jimmy's missing BMX. The sight of it jolted me further back than his funeral or wake, right to the day I found him dead. Since Jimmy's death my life had been like a haunted Ghost Train, with fluorescent skeletons and creaking coffins. It was the hanging rags which brushed my face that scared me the most though — the bike was an unforeseeable haunting. Instinctively I tried the passenger handle but it was locked.

Before I could say anything Cora pulled my arm to follow her. "Anthony, we've mystery guests in the pub."

The Elm Tree's open door drew us in and we followed Phil into the lounge, my eyes darting from man to man, recognising no one. There was the low hum of conversation. Round-bellied men with balding heads were clustered at a wooden table, hands clutching glasses on beer mats. A group of younger men threw darts at a board, and puffed cigarettes. In the corner sat a young man with thick auburn hair.

"Hello Tony, it's good to see you," said a man next to me, slender with freckled skin and brown eyes.

For a second I wondered if I was on *Candid Camera,* that the last few months of my life had been a joke and any time now Jimmy would appear with a *gotcha* look on his face, but there was no microphone in the man's hand.

"I'm Michael, Michael Bray." His wheaten hair stuck straight up and waved in all directions. He was wearing a brown suede coat. "My son and I have come from Warwickshire to see you today."

I followed Michael Bray's gaze to the auburn-haired stranger. Another Bray?

Cora touched my shoulder. "Anthony, come and sit down."

Phil ordered a pint of bitter and two colas while Michael and Cora led me to the table in the corner.

The young man stood, offered me a handshake and in an English accent said, "Good to meet you Tony, my name's David Bray."

"Jimmy's cousin," said Cora.

"Cousin? The one who wrote to Jimmy with all the music news?"

David nodded and smiled.

"Finally. It's good to meet you there, David." I shook his hand, relieved that the suspense was over, and we all sat.

"I hear you had quite a journey to England."

"Yes, it was a bit unexpected but Ireland's too quiet without Cora."

Cora leaned her head on my arm. David smiled and my eyes locked with his as they had with Dominic O'Leary. There was certainty then, that we would be friends no matter what followed.

eleven

The barman put a fizzing cola drink on the bar and opened the fridge for lemonade.

"I wonder if David knows that Jimmy is only his half cousin."

"I doubt it," replied Cora. "Are you going to tell him?"

"Does he need to know?"

Cora shook her head then took a sip of her cola, blinking when bubbles popped in her face. I smiled inside.

On the bench next to David, Michael Bray took the change from me and dropped it into his jacket pocket. By the cut of his clothes I took him to be younger than Mr Bray. He was explaining their circumstances to Phil. "Sadly my wife died last summer; it was a terrible shock, cancer."

David looked to Michael who winked at him affectionately. "My dad went across to Jimmy's funeral, where you spotted his car, Tony," said David. "There was no way I could go, because it would mean taking a break from school. When Dad came back from Jimmy's funeral he brought Jimmy's bike with him for me. Jimmy knew I loved his bike."

"How? Did you see pictures?" I asked.

"No, when Mum died my dad needed a break," said David, "I went to Barley Cove to spend a week with the Brays during the school holidays. It was the only time I spent with Jimmy, but we were like brothers that week. I'm sorry I didn't get to meet you then, Tony. Jimmy talked about you a lot though, told me how you'd done up his bike. His BMX is yours now. We'll get it shipped back to Ireland if need be."

For the first time I thought I knew what having an older brother must be like. "What did you like the most about Ireland when you were there?" I asked him.

"The fishing, without a doubt. Did you know Jimmy could catch a salmon with his bare hands?"

Cora and I turned to each other at the same time.

"Are you okay?" asked David.

"You're the one Mr Callaghan saw Jimmy with! He said he'd seen Jimmy fishing with someone last summer but didn't know who. It was you!"

"It must have been," said David.

"It's odd that Jimmy never mentioned your visit," I said.

David's eyes flitted around everyone at the table.

The barman reached an arm between Cora and me, and chinked three empty glasses together before lifting them away.

Phil intervened. "Let's go back to the house for some privacy shall we?"

The men led the way with Cora.

David waited for me. "Cora said on the phone she'd asked around at church until someone told her where she could find Mr Bray's brother. She made everyone keep it a secret we were coming here today."

"It's all there's been recently, secrets," I said.

"You must have had enough."

I nodded.

"I think I know why Jimmy didn't tell you about my visit, Tony," David stood and faced me, his hands in his trouser pockets. "When I got to Ireland last August Jimmy listened about my mum dying and I'm not ashamed to say that I cried in front of him. He started crying too and asked if any of my uncles ever messed with me." David rubbed his eyes. "I said no, of course not!"

"What do you mean? Did Tom hit Jimmy?" I asked.

"Worse than that." David looked away. "He told me that his uncle had…?"

It came as a deluge, the thought of what Tom had done to my mate Jimmy. I staggered backwards and sat on number sixteen's low front wall. I remembered something he'd told once when he said he didn't want to ride Millie. He looked in pain and I asked him what was wrong. He looked away and mumbled, 'it feels like I'm shitting fire'. Now I understood why he looked so ashamed, why he changed the subject when I asked if he'd seen the doctor. I'd forgotten his words until this moment, when it made horrible, tragic sense. I cursed and cursed again. My friend had been assaulted in the worst way and I hadn't helped him, hadn't even understood.

"He made me swear not to tell anyone," David said.

"There was a day last summer that Tom O'Leary delivered peat to the farm. Jimmy wouldn't help him unload the truck but went to the barn instead. Tom followed him in, and I went home. That day has stuck in my head, and now I know why."

"None of this is your fault, Tony. His mother was making him visit Tom and made him swear not to tell anyone."

Because Tom was his father, I thought.

"When I got back to England I wanted to talk to my mum so bad. I ended up phoning the *Samaritans* because I couldn't get Jimmy's secret out of my head. They suggested Jimmy phone them, so I wrote to him."

"Jimmy told me he'd heard from you. You sent a magazine, I remember looking at it with Jimmy."

"That's right, I thought it would lighten things a bit. He never replied though, and the Bray's don't have a phone." David sat next to me on the wall. "I wish I'd told my dad."

"You kept your promise to Jimmy not to tell a soul and he might have phoned the *Samaritans* from a phone box – we'll never know."

"It wasn't enough to save him," said David, rolling a stone under his shoe.

My hands were shaking, my top lip damp with sweat. I pulled off my sweater. "David, I have to tell you something, and it's not very nice."

David blinked as he registered that it was Jimmy's shocking discovery about Tom that had led him to his death.

Cora twitched the net curtain in the front window and giggled when we caught her spying.

"She's a cracking girl," said Michael, dropping my bag onto the back seat of his car.

I nodded.

"You make sure you keep in touch, Tony," Christine said. "Remember, you're welcome to come and stay for however long you want."

I crouched down and the twins both hugged me at the same time. "You be good for your mammy now," I said.

Cora appeared from the entry. We had said our goodbyes in the house and I made her promise not to come outside. She gave me a kiss on the cheek. "Don't be a stranger."

With David in the back, Michael opened the passenger side for me, and Cora, Christine, Phil and the children stood back on the pavement. Michael started the engine.

I wound down the window. "Look after Jimmy's bike," I called.

"We will. Don't forget to phone when you get back home," shouted Christine.

I waved and Cora blew kisses before the car moved off, turned left at The Elm, and headed down Nottingham Road.

twelve

My parents collected me from Cork airport. Mam looked frail, the colour in her eyes faded. We drove home in silence with the familiar smell of peat wafting through the car's vents.

Dad slowed and wound down a window to greet one of Barley Cove's old men waving his stick in our direction

"Are you well?" my father asked him.

"Aye. The priest though, he's dying so he is."

"Father Molony?" Mam said leaning over to the window.

"On his deathbed, sure enough."

"We'll be over there after a cup of tea," said Mam.

Mam was on the phone to Beth as soon as we arrived home. Upstairs my room smelled stale and I opened the window. One of the corners on my *Quadrophenia* poster was peeled away from the wall and I tried sticking the poster corner down again, but a gust of wind caught the glossy paper and yanked it from the wall. I left it on the floor and flopped onto the bed. I missed Cora already.

An hour later I heard Beth's heels on the path outside. They were going to see the priest and I was going with them. In the bathroom I splashed water on my face and patted it with a towel before rushing downstairs.

"I'm coming with you!" I announced.

"Tony, good to see you back," said Beth.

Beth diverted her eyes. She knew something, and she knew I knew.

"Tony, it's an awful sad thing where we're going,

will you not stay home with your Dad?"

"Don't patronise me, Mam, I'm coming."

"Well, there's a word you must have learned in England." The women chuckled.

Father Molony's housekeeper let us in and the smell of sickness ran up my nostrils. The women took seats, one either side of the bed-bound priest, speaking in whispers and stroking his hands. Father Molony's eyes were closed, his lips dry and cracked. The colour of his face was grey, as if someone had turned a television dial from colour to black and white. Over the priest's head was the red glow of the Lord's presence, a flickering candle before a picture of the *Sacred Heart*. The faded floral wall paper curled from the corners where it was supposed to meet the ceiling. Next to the brass bedstead was an open Bible, a gold ribbon marking a page. The dresser held brown medicine bottles and a bowl of water with a flannel over its edge. The housekeeper brought Mam and Beth tea before she mopped the priest's brow and plumped his pillows. Only when dusk fell along the grassed front-garden did my mother and Beth say their goodbyes. I asked if I could be alone with the priest for a last confession and the women agreed, treading lightly as they left.

Father Molony's eyes opened briefly and he smiled before closing them again. "Tony Barber, have you come to say goodbye?"

"I have, Father," I replied. "I've been to England."

"I know, boy, you have been a worry to your family."

"I know Tom O'Leary was Jimmy's father."

The priest's closed eyes twitched under his furrowed brow.

"I'm sorry for stealing the bottle of whiskey from the Brays but it wasn't me who killed Tom O'Leary, Father.

He really was dead when we got there."

The priest said nothing and I worried he'd speak no more but he looked at me again, his lips drawn into a straight smile, his eyes soft. "I know, son, and I shouldn't have let you think it was your fault."

"How do you know?"

Father Molony grabbed my hand and pulled me closer. His voice wheezed: "The night he died he was an animal with the drink, an evil Jekyll and Hyde. He wanted to tell the village he was Jimmy's father and I couldn't let him do it." Father Molony coughed and his breathing became laboured. "I pushed him back into the kitchen with his arms flailing. He bit me in the arm and with the pain I struck out." The priest's chest heaved up and down. "Tom's head hit the stove. He was probably dead before he hit the ground." The priest crossed himself and his breathing gradually slowed. He looked at me and squeezed my hand. "There you are, Tony Barber, it was me who killed Tom O'Leary."

Father Molony kept my hand and I cupped his. The weight of guilt which hung about me disappeared. No one murdered Tom O'Leary. He would have died from the bottle alone in the end, in a pool of vomit rather than a pool of blood. The last of the light faded, and the priest's cheeks glistened in the shadows. Walking to the basin, I dipped the face cloth into the cool water and wrung it out, then wiped Father Molony's tears and said a prayer for his soul.

thirteen

There was a flicker in Dominic O'Leary's window, welcoming on the dark hill. Amy barked when I tapped. Dominic's hair was out of its band, long over his shoulders. "You've come."

Inside the hearth crackled, and even in April's mild temperature, Dominic's hut felt cool and still. He moved the kettle over the flames. On Dominic's small work table was an acorn, carved from pale wood.

"The priest is on his deathbed," said Dominic, setting up the tea pot.

"I've been to see him."

"And?"

"I'd say tonight's his last."

"He's not been right since brother Tom died." Dominic looked me in the eye and it happened again, the transference of knowledge which didn't need to be said.

"I've company coming tonight, Tony. She won't be surprised to see you, I heard from her you'd been with the priest."

"Beth?"

"Beth."

We drank strong tea and Dominic picked up his carving, smoothing the knife around the grain. Amy dozed in front of the fire, her eyes opening gently when shavings fell to the floor.

Beth entered without knocking and Amy stood and gave a sharp bark. Dominic poured Beth a drink and Amy's tail wagged before she sat. Beth lifted a chair from the beneath the table and joined us around the hearth. The room was dark, and licking flames showed us wisps of hair on Beth's neck, fallen from her pins. Her whiskey and water cradled by willowy fingers, delicate against a chunky glass. "Father Molony is in a poor way," she said.

"He's sick, so he is," said Dominic. "Tony said tonight'll be his last."

"Could well be," she said. "That's three we'll have lost from the village in the last six months." Beth shuffled on her seat, and watched the flames for a while. "Tony, did you know I delivered Jimmy when he was born?"

"No. I didn't."

"He's the only baby I've delivered who didn't cry." She smiled. "His mother said he made up for it over the years with his constant chatter."

"He was friendly he was," said Dominic. "Everyone loved him."

There was an expectant silence, like when the bells tinkle before Mass and everyone hushes, knowing the priest will emerge with the altar boys behind him. Dominic took a deep breath and I picked at the skin around my thumb nail. My thoughts raced to the promise Jimmy asked David Bray to keep. The promise I had decided not to tell Cora, to spare her the awfulness of what Tom had done to a young man she was fond of.

Dominic said, "We'll go outside, get some air."

Amy plodded behind me as I followed Beth. Between the branches the sky was flecked with reds and creams, the light had dimmed and the birds were singing. Dominic looked over the cove and Beth walked slowly, away from the canopy of trees towards the open hillside.

Dominic turned to face me. "You met Jimmy's cousin in England."

"Yes, we got on very well."

"You'll be thinking of going back to England then."

"When I'm sixteen. There's a chance I could do my A'levels over there."

Dominic smiled. "Your education's important. How will you support yourself?"

"Cora's cousins have said I can stay with them, and I can get a Saturday job."

"Will you marry the American?"

"One day, maybe."

Dominic gave a small chuckle. There would be talk, if my parents agreed to me going back to England to live with Cora. Mam had said she would consider it. It was the only way she could convince me to come back to Ireland to finish my school year.

The patterns in the sky were like a tablecloth being pulled from the table, its streaks of colour fading to a triangle. Tom O'Leary's house was in darkness, with no smoke coming from its chimney. He would be buried in the same graveyard as Jimmy, but to me the house below would be his tomb. The pebble beach beyond, where Cora and I waited for Tom to fall asleep was where I'd go with Jimmy sometimes and skim stones into the waves.

"Cora couldn't live with me here now," I continued. "Only Jimmy's ghost is here. Sometimes I think I hear him laughing."

"He's happy where he is." Dominic nodded his head slowly.

"What happened when he died?"

Dominic crouched and picked up a pine cone, removing brown pine needles and moss from it. He bounced it in his hand like a ball, and Amy locked her stare on it.

"The night Jimmy died his mother went to Tom O'Leary." Dominic looked down towards Tom's house. "She told him she'd found her son dead, with a bottle of her pills half empty by his bed."

"What did Tom do?" I asked.

"Tom came to me, Tony, and asked me to help get rid of the body."

"What!"

"'Tis true. When I got up there Jimmy's mother was hysterical. She kept moaning how Jimmy had brought shame on the family, how their livelihood would be ruined."

My legs felt as if the blood was turning to red quivering ribbons. "Didn't she care that Jimmy was dead?"

"That I don't know, I suppose she must." Dominic threw the pine cone into the bracken below and Amy pounced to the edge of the ledge in search of it. "Mr Bray was away and my sister and Tom were desperate to get Jimmy's body out of the house before her husband came home and found out the truth." Dominic picked up a twig and Amy returned to him, watching as he snapped it and picked at the bark. "I left them at the farm saying I wouldn't have anything to do with it. Then I heard Jimmy had been found in the river and I knew what they'd done." He threw part of the stick and Amy ran after it. She picked it up delicately and chewed a little, bits of bark dropping from her mouth.

An image came of Mrs Bray holding Jimmy under his arms, as Dad had held me when I fell in the river after finding Jimmy; and Tom O'Leary holding Jimmy's legs as if to give him a *leg and a wing*. The image popped away, like a blown lamp bulb, and spared me the thought of seeing Jimmy land in the water. "God almighty," I muttered. "Who's idea was that?"

"Not mine, for sure. I should have got the doctor up there as quick."

Amy ran towards the clearing and Beth came into view. Dominic looked out over the cove again as if closing the pages of a half-read book. Beth put her hand on his shoulder and he wiped his eyes before turning round. "He knows how Jimmy got into the river, Beth."

A bird unsettled a branch above before flying away.

"I don't understand," I said. The inquest showed death by drowning; there was water in his lungs."

Dominic spoke. "After I left the farm, Tom went to Beth and said one of his calves was sick with mucus and did she have anything from the hospital to save him calling out the vet."

"I gave him tubing from a catheter thinking it wouldn't hurt the calf," said Beth. "He used it to pump river water into Jimmy's lungs."

I grabbed my nose in defence of the sensation of a tube being pushed up it. I walked away from them both, into the clearing, and to the path that followed to the Harrington's. The sky was getting darker but I my eyesight was keen and if I'd have been an eagle I could have swooped at that moment and caught my prey with no difficulty. There was an urge to run, down the path to the road, grab my bag and leave for good. That night though, I was the prey, and had to endure the attack before breaking free. I turned around, away from the path, back under the canopy of trees to Dominic and Beth. They were in an embrace.

"Hello, girl," I said to Amy, to let them know I was there.

"It's understandable you're upset," said Beth, my mother's trusted and caring friend.

"Does my mam know?" I asked her.

Dominic answered. "No, she knows Beth and I are talking is all."

Beth nodded in agreement. "We've been living in fear ever since you found Jimmy," she said.

"When Jimmy was found dead," Dominic continued, "Beth came to see me and we talked for the first time in years. Beth mentioned Tom coming to see her the night before. It didn't take me long to figure out what they'd done. I told Beth to keep quiet about it or we'd be drawn in." Dominic put a hand on Beth's arm; she wiped under her eyes, breathed in deeply and put her hand over Dominic's.

"We know what they did was wrong," she said, "but Jimmy's mother is in poor health and if this gets out she'll break down completely. She might try and follow Jimmy. Two people have lost their lives already because of brother Tom."

"I found the catheter tubing at Tom's the night Cora and I searched for clues,' I told them. "It was odd Tom keeping that in a dresser drawer."

"So you know we're telling the truth," said Beth, her eyes filled with tears again.

"Let's go in," said Dominic. "You can walk home with Beth when she's finished her drink."

Amy yawned and rested her chin over her paws. The fire crackled. Mam; trying to keep secret Beth was talking to Dominic again; if only that's all there was to hide. No amount of hope, prayer or chicken soup would bring Jimmy back.

Our voices were hushed by the presence of the truth. All was still, like the sand in an hour glass which has finished pouring through time, and I wondered, what would Cora be doing now?

I picked up the extension in my room and dialled Cora's number. It rang three times.

"Hello. Seven one eight, five four five." It was

Christine.

"Christine, hello it's Tony."

"Tony, how are you? Did you get home safely?"

"It was a good trip and all is well thank you."

"That's great. Are you still thinking about coming to Nottingham?"

"Yes, once I've got my exams out of the way. I've convinced Mam I'll do better at the sixth form college there."

"Ah that's grand."

"Is Cora there please?"

"She's standing right here next to me." The phone sounded as if it was being stuffed into a plastic bag, and then Cora's voice.

"Anthony!"

"Cora!"

"I was worried, why didn't you phone to say you got back okay?"

"Cora, so much has happened," and I told her about Father Molony, Beth and Dominic. I told her how Jimmy had found his way to the water, and how Tom had met his death. Cora spoke softly when my tears came, allowing me to turn away from the phone until I could talk again.